General editor: Graham Handley MA PhD

Brodie's Notes on Thomas Hardy's
The Mayor of Casterbridge

David Scholar
Head of English, Enfield Chace School

MACMILLAN

This revised edition first published 1986
by Pan Books Ltd

Published 1992 by
MACMILLAN PRESS LTD
Houndmills, Basingstoke, Hampshire RG21 6XS
and London
Companies and representatives
throughout the world

ISBN 0–333–58117–2

10 9 8 7 6 5 4 3 2
03 02 01 00 99 98 97 96 95

Printed in Great Britain by
Cox and Wyman Ltd
Reading, Berkshire

Contents

Page references in these Notes are to the Pan
edition of *The Mayor of Casterbridge*, but as
references are also given to particular chapters,
the Notes may be used with any edition of the book.

Preface by the general editor

The intention throughout this study aid is to stimulate and guide, to encourage your involvement in the book, and to develop informed responses and a sure understanding of the main details.

Brodie's Notes provide a clear outline of the play or novel's plot, followed by act, scene, or chapter summaries and/or commentaries. These are designed to emphasize the most important literary and factual details. Poems, stories or non-fiction texts combine brief summary with critical commentary on individual aspects or common features of the genre being examined. Textual notes define what is difficult or obscure and emphasize literary qualities. Revision questions are set at appropriate points to test your ability to appreciate the prescribed book and to write accurately and relevantly about it.

In addition, each of these Notes includes a critical appreciation of the author's art. This covers such major elements as characterization, style, structure, setting and themes. Poems are examined technically – rhyme, rhythm, for instance. In fact, any important aspect of the prescribed work will be evaluated. The aim is to send you back to the text you are studying.

Each study aid concludes with a series of general questions which require a detailed knowledge of the book: some of these questions may invite comparison with other books, some will be suitable for coursework exercises, and some could be adapted to work you are doing on another book or books. Each study aid has been adapted to meet the needs of the current examination requirements. They provide a basic, individual and imaginative response to the work being studied, and it is hoped that they will stimulate you to acquire disciplined reading habits and critical fluency.

Graham Handley 1991

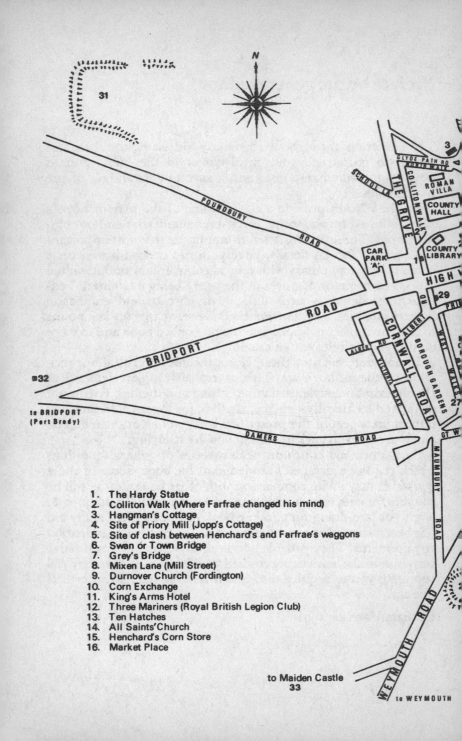

N

31

GLYDE PATH RO

SCHOOL LA

THE GROVE

COLLITONWALK

3

ROMAN VILLA

COUNTY HALL

POUNDBURY ROAD

CAR PARK 'A'

COUNTY LIBRARY

18

HIGH W

29

ROAD

CORNWALL ROAD

ALBERT

PRI

WEST

ROAD

BRIDPORT ROAD

ALBER RD

VICTORIA RD

BOROUGH GARDENS

27

■32

to BRIDPORT
(Port Bredy)

DAMERS ROAD

GT W

MAUMBURY ROAD

WEYMOUTH ROAD

to Maiden Castle
33

to WEYMOUTH

1. The Hardy Statue
2. Colliton Walk (Where Farfrae changed his mind)
3. Hangman's Cottage
4. Site of Priory Mill (Jopp's Cottage)
5. Site of clash between Henchard's and Farfrae's waggons
6. Swan or Town Bridge
7. Grey's Bridge
8. Mixen Lane (Mill Street)
9. Durnover Church (Fordington)
10. Corn Exchange
11. King's Arms Hotel
12. Three Mariners (Royal British Legion Club)
13. Ten Hatches
14. All Saints' Church
15. Henchard's Corn Store
16. Market Place

Dorchester

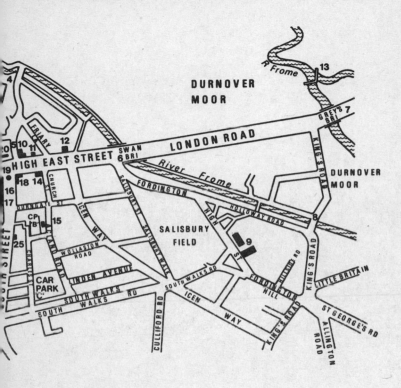

The author and his work

Thomas Hardy was born on 2 June 1840, the eldest child of a master mason (or builder) of the village of Upper Bockhampton, in the parish of Stinsford, near Dorchester. His father was comfortably off but unambitious. His business was a good one for the village. He employed no fewer than fifteen men at one time, including his neighbour the tranter, who carried all his building materials. Things in the village were much as Hardy describes them in *Under the Greenwood Tree*. This secluded and self-contained community was as yet, unaffected by the machine age, though the railway came to Dorchester when Hardy was seven years old.

As a child Hardy was precocious but delicate, and he had no formal schooling until he was eight. First he went to the village school at Lower Bockhampton (Fancy Day's school in *Under the Greenwood Tree*) and a year later to a private school in Dorchester. He worked hard and became a good all rounder in his studies, showing a particular aptitude for Latin. He was a shy boy, very much in earnest. In his leisure time his father taught him to play the violin and prepare manuscript music for himself. One of his first presents from his father was a toy accordion. His father was a fiddler in the west gallery of Stinsford Church Choir, one much in demand at country festivals. Hardy's father, grandfather and great-grandfather had all been in the choir and master-masons in Stinsford; it was a coveted hereditary honour in the family. After school and in the holidays his father often took the boy with him when he was playing at weddings and parties in the neighbourhood. Hardy's mother was an omnivorous reader, who took good care to see that her son read well, for example Dryden's *Virgil* and Dr Johnson's *Rasselas*. She had taught him to read by the time he was three. She was a good singer too, and he loved the old ballads that she used to sing to him. The tune '*Miss M'Leod of Ayr*' (See Chapter 16) was one he learned from his mother.

At the age of twenty Hardy went into the offices of an ecclesiastical architect in Dorchester; his master, John Hicks, was an educated man and a competent classical scholar. Young

Thomas pursued his studies when working hours were over and taught himself Greek as well as improving his Latin. Speaking of his life at this time, Hardy wrote of 'the professional life, the scholar's life and the rustic life combined in the twenty-four hours of the day'. To this period belong a few poems, but they were not published. His work as an architect's pupil was always his first concern, for Hardy never undertook anything to which he could not give of his best.

In 1862 Hardy went to London as a 'young Gothic draughts-man who could restore and design churches and rectory houses', in the office of A. W. Blomfield, a leading London architect. In the same year he won the RIBA essay prize. He followed this up by winning the Institute's prize and medal the next year. Some eight years later, together with another architect, Hardy had his designs for schools accepted in a competition arranged by the London School Board. His first published work was in *Chambers Journal* in March 1865: 'How I Built myself a House', a gently ironic piece, easily written. Hardy's knowledge of architecture is repeatedly shown in *The Mayor of Casterbridge*.

All this time Hardy was becoming more and more interested in literature – not only in the classics of English Literature, but in the exciting contemporary publications of the 1860s. He thought seriously on what he read; he never accepted anything lightly. He had also developed an interest in art and at one time intended to become an art critic. There are many references to art in *The Mayor of Casterbridge* e.g. to Correggio (Chapter 16), Titian (22), or the Tuscan school (26).

In 1867 Hardy returned to Dorchester as an assistant to his old principal architect Mr Hicks. It was now, back at home, that he started to write fiction. His first effort was not accepted and the second, *Desperate Remedies*, rejected by Macmillan (later to be his publishers), was accepted only at his own risk by a lesser known house. He lost financially, as copies of the novel had to be remaindered; but he had the satisfaction of seeing his work in print.

Setbacks can be more significant than successes, however, and the young novelist now realized where his skill lay – not in sensational incident but in description of the Dorset countryside and people; he set about writing *Under the Greenwood Tree*. Early in 1871 he was back at Bockhampton once more, among the scenes of his boyhood. In 1872 the novel was accepted by

Tinsley Bros at their risk; they paid £30 for the copyright. Hardy did not feel confident enough in 1872 to publish under his own name, and no wonder, for the *Spectator* reviewer of *Desperate Remedies* welcomed an anonymity that would save disgrace to the family name. Further, if he let his employers know that he spent his time writing novels, and unsuccessful ones at that, it might affect his business reputation. Hardy need not have feared. *Under the Greenwood Tree*, if not an immediate success, was no failure, here or in America the next year.

The secret had leaked out in the publishing world: one day Hardy received a letter from the new Editor of the *Cornhill Magazine*, saying that he had much admired the freshness of *Under the Greenwood Tree*, and enquiring if Hardy would write a serial for the *Cornhill*. He was too busy at that time writing *A Pair of Blue Eyes* for *Tinsley's Magazine*, but promised his next work. The result was *Far from the Madding Crowd*, which was published in serial form in the Cornhill throughout 1874. It was an immediate success and was published no fewer than seven times in its first year: in the *Cornhill* anonymously; as a complete volume separately in England and the USA in November; and in four American magazines. *Far from the Madding Crowd* turned out to be Hardy's best seller after *Tess of the d'Urbervilles*.

Hardy now felt quite safe in giving up work as an architect for good, and married a Cornish woman of his own age whom he had met over four years before while doing architectural work on a church Hicks had been instructed to restore. It was she who, in 1871, when he was disappointed, encouraged him to stick to literature. Hardy's retiring nature is shown in his quiet wedding. Only two witnesses were present, nobody from his family. At first the couple were happy, but their opposite dispositions and characters eventually brought them to lead separate lives. Hardy and his wife were not close in feeling, and the lack of inspiration in their marriage may have been one reason for the growing gloom and pessimism of his later novels. After *Far from the Madding Crowd* Hardy went from success to success (though not all his novels met with popular approval): *The Return of the Native* (1878); *The Trumpet-Major* (1880); *The Mayor of Casterbridge* (1886), first issued as a serial in *The Graphic*.

In 1883 Hardy and his wife went back to Dorchester and rented accommodation near the Shire Hall while he saw to the building of the house he had decided on. The town provided just the stimulus he needed, and he was elected a Justice of the Peace, which may well have helped him in the picture of local government that is worked into this novel. There is evidence that he consulted the *Dorset County Chronicle* extensively while writing it, and he was able to work the fabric of the town into the fabric of the book. After *The Mayor of Casterbridge* came *The Woodlanders* (1887), *Tess of the d'Urbervilles* (1891) and *Jude the Obscure* (1894). The last, so out of keeping with Victorian senti- ment, was attacked so fiercely that Hardy decided once and for all that he would write no more novels. Instead at his house Max Gate, which had been finished in 1885, he returned to poetry.

In 1912 his wife died. It is strangely ironic that the loss of a partner to whom he had apparently been indifferent for many years should serve to release from him a series of poems so passionate that it is hard to believe that the relationship had been sterile for so long. In his old age he married Miss Florence Dugdale, an author of children's stories – an Enfield woman of Dorset stock, who had often helped him with his writing when his eyes were bad and had looked up material for him in the Library of the British Museum. There was nearly forty years' difference in age between them, but her love, devotion, admir- ation and unceasing care made his last years supremely happy. She became one of his first biographers, though there is strong evidence that the book she wrote was written in collaboration with him and that together they concealed anything that he did not wish to be known. Hardy lived a quiet life, and described himself as aloof rather than shy. His pleasures were simple, and not until he became too infirm to cycle would he buy a car.

Acknowledged as the greatest living English novelist, Hardy had reached this position with no regular school and university education, but now three universities were happy to honour him (and themselves) by awarding him the honorary degree of D.Litt. Hardy tried to ward off would-be admirers, could never be persuaded to talk about himself, and shrank from making speeches. The honour he appreciated most was the Freedom of Dorchester – more even than the Order of Merit with which he was invested in the same year (1910). Hardy's last public appear- ance was in 1927, when he laid the foundation stone of the new buildings of Dorchester Grammar School, of which he had been a governor for many years. His love of music continued to the end, and his violin and cello always stood in a corner by the bookcase in his study. His works were constantly reprinted and he left a fortune of nearly £100,000. He died on 11 January 1928.

The irony which pervades much of Hardy's work was given a dramatic twist after his death. It was decided that the man who had never sought fame should be buried in Westminster Abbey; there were quarrels over precedence for tickets, and the Prime Minister was among the illustrious who bore the pall. The avowed agnostic was buried in England's national shrine. The body was cremated and the ashes interred in Poets' Corner, next to Dickens's grave, with a spadeful of Dorset earth thrown over. But his heart was carried back to Stinsford, where it was buried in the grave of his first wife.

Plot, source and setting

Plot

The story arises from a hay-trusser's volatile temper and love of drink together with his great energy and capacity for hard work. Arriving at a fair while looking for work, Michael Henchard is led to drink too much and, while under the influence, sells his wife and little daughter to a sailor. Returning to his senses next morning he makes a solemn vow not to touch strong drink for twenty-one years. All his efforts to find his wife fail.

Henchard settles in Casterbridge and by his energy and flair builds up a good corn business, in time becoming Mayor of the town. Exactly eighteen years later his wife returns with her daughter, supposing her sailor 'husband' to be dead. Henchard and she keep their relationship secret; he courts her and marries her again. His business grows in size and prosperity under the capable management of a young Scot, Donald Farfrae. However, Henchard quarrels with Farfrae, who sets up on his own and soon becomes a formidable rival. Mrs Henchard dies. Henchard finds out that her daughter, whom he had thought was his own (and whom he had so informed), is in fact the sailor's daughter, as his own had died.

Farfrae rises as Henchard falls. He marries the woman (Lucetta) Henchard expects to marry; he buys his business when Henchard goes bankrupt and lives in his house. Henchard's degradation is complete when his past becomes known and he takes to drink once more – the twenty-one years of his vow having passed.

Henchard's stepdaughter, whom he had at first treated roughly when he discovered that she was not his, in due time wins her way to his heart and turns out to be his only comfort in life. However, Elizabeth-Jane is now claimed by the sailor (Newson), who comes to Casterbridge to find her, and she is disgusted by Henchard's deceit in concealing her parentage from her. Finally she marries Farfrae, whose wife has died; Henchard turns his back on the town and comes to a wretched end in a tumbledown cottage.

Source

Hardy's main source for the *Mayor of Casterbridge* was the town he knew so well, and which is as important as the Mayor himself in the part it plays. There is no doubt that many of the characters Hardy describes were subtly altered versions of real people; but the real source of his story lies in the tales he heard his mother tell of her childhood. While he was working on the *Mayor* he read extensively among the back numbers of the *Dorset County Chronicle* for the years 1820–1835, and in them set out as factual reportage, one can find the wife-selling, living with a second husband, public dinners at the 'King's Arms', Henchard's generous conduct at his bankruptcy, his oath to abstain from drink and his behaviour towards Abel Whittle.

Farfrae is a Scot as seen by a southerner – which means that to a real Scot he would not appear at all convincing. But in Dorchester a Yorkshireman named Eddison established a factory for making steam ploughs in the 1860s and it had an impact on the town comparable to that made by Farfrae. Reference has already been made to the opening of Portland Harbour breakwater by the Prince Regent in 1849, when he passed through Dorchester on the way here.

Hardy's achievement is that he has worked all these different threads together to make a convincing story; none of these elements is in itself remarkable.

Setting

Hardy's novels are an unusual blend of fact and fiction; if the story itself is ultimately fiction, it is solidly founded on fact and this is nowhere more evident than in the settings given to his novels.

The Mayor of Casterbridge opens at Weydon-Priors, the modern Weyhill and formerly the site of one of the biggest fairs in Southern England, mentioned in *Piers Plowman* and by Cobbett as well as by Hardy. It was in decline throughout the nineteenth century, a decline which Hardy chronicles between Henchard's first visit there and Susan Henchard's eighteen years later. This basis of fact is one of the most fascinating features of *The Mayor of Casterbridge* for it means that one can walk around the town of Dorchester and see the exact location of many of the incidents described. The house which was imagined as being first Henchard's then Farfrae's, now Barclays Bank, has even had a blue plaque fixed to it, and its fictional former residents have become more real to most people than its factual ones are ever likely to be. If the granaries and garden behind the house are now a municipal car park, the warehouse, with its beam for hoisting sacks, that is the imagined setting for the fight with Farfrae, is still there. To find High-Place Hall is rather harder: the curious visitor will not find it where it is described, as confronting the main market-place; in fact it is in a side street perhaps four hundred metres away in the north-west quarter of the town, and Hardy's imagination has moved it to the site it occupies in the novel.

If then the fictional Casterbridge differs in some respects from the factual Dorchester, and if Dorchester in the twentieth century has changed less than many other English towns of comparable size, Hardy himself would note tremendous changes, as the town he describes was, even when he wrote the novel in 1884, passing away; we hear several times in footnotes of buildings 'since demolished'. He was drawing on his memories of the town as it was when he was a boy. He had been to school in Dorchester, and at the age of twenty he had started work there in an architect's office, so his descriptions of the town combine affection with close knowledge. The description of the 'Three Mariners' in Chapters 6 and 7, of Henchard's house, and the aspects of the town seen by Elizabeth-Jane in Chapter 9, to name but three instances, are examples of this affectionate portraiture that is so much a part of the novel. The life of a town is fluid, and to give it any sense of completeness it needs to be shown as part of a slowly changing historical entity and at different times of the year. One is always aware of the history of Casterbridge. It is emphasized particularly in the episodes centred on the Ring, the Roman amphitheatre and centre of medieval and modern entertainments, and in one's awareness that the street pattern of the town exactly follows that of the Roman town built fifteen hundred years before. The novel opens in late summer; after a gap of eighteen years the talk is still of the quality of the corn. Next morning one hears of the imminent autumn. Later on spring comes with a hiring fair and a new seed drill. Susan and Elizabeth-Jane arrive in the evening; Elizabeth Jane takes her walk in the early morning.

One can never fail to be aware that the life of Casterbridge is intimately bound up with that of the agricultural community around it. The goods sold in the shops are those of which a farming community stands in need, and the shops and inns stay open as long as there is a chance of customers. The business of the market is done in the streets: 'The farmers as a rule preferred the open *carrefour* for their transactions, despite its inconvenient jostlings and the danger from crossing vehicles, to the gloomy sheltered market-room prepared for them'. Life goes on at a much slower pace than it does today. People's lives have a leisurely air, even though men had to work for long hours, normally a ten hour day, not including meal breaks – they went out early in the morning and returned home in time for breakfast. Farfrae sets out before six; a waggoner starts work at six and if his employer tells him to be there at four he is at his employer's mercy and likely to be without a job at all unless he complies. For this he earned eight shillings a week.

The ordinary people of the town appear in a number of ways. Hardy shows Abel Whittle as typical of the ordinary labourer – unable to read, his great weakness an inability to get up in the morning. Others are characterized by the chorus that Hardy uses to comment on the events of the story from time to time – they process from church to the 'Three Mariners' and one of whom is practical realist enough to take the pennies from Susan Henchard's eyes and spend them on beer.

New ideas come to Casterbridge late. Farfrae, who by his introduction of a new seed drill is seen by Henchard as stupid, is introducing ideas that are commonplace in other parts of the country and at the start his technique of restoring bad corn is unknown in the town. In fact a native of Leeds had started a factory that made steam ploughs in Dorchester in the 1870s only to see, after a decade of prosperity, the market collapse and the firm threatened with bankruptcy before it adapted by changing to other products.

In a town where few ever left it unless they walked, it is clear that life revolved around local gossip. The occasional celebration like Farfrae's or Henchard's entertainment, the arrival of a royal personality or a noted wedding were exceptional; the more usual entertainment of the townspeople appears in the novel as recent or legendary tales like those of bear baitings or public executions, or more practically in the occasional skimmity ride, which is frowned on by the authorities and hugely enjoyed by the participants.

Outside the Walks the town gives way to fields and rich cornland, woods and open downland and heath cut by dusty roads. Lastly, one can never forget the weather of *The Mayor of Casterbridge*; it has a direct effect on many of the events of the novel and seems then as now sometimes a force at best indifferent to man, sometimes actively hostile towards him. It is partly to try to understand such things that people visit the weather prophet Mr Fall, knowing it is superstitious to do so yet not fully able to believe it is pointless. The attitude of most people in the story towards the Church and religion would seem to have much in common with this, as exemplified by the use Henchard makes of the church in swearing his oath.

Structure and themes

Structure

The structure is a most important part of any novel; indeed the novelist's main task is to decide on his structure; once he has done so, the actual writing is relatively straightforward. The structure of *The Mayor of Casterbridge* is simple in that it is the story of one man: it starts by describing him as an ambitious if headstrong hay-trusser looking for work; it ends with his death.

After a quiet sombre start the story becomes suddenly tense and melodramatic. In contrast with the popular conception of the Victorian novel, which spends the first few chapters introducing characters and setting the scene, Henchard has sold his wife by the end of Chapter 1. Together with Chapter 2, which deals with his attempts to find her again, it may be regarded as a prologue to the main action because it is separated from it by eighteen years. From Chapter 3 onwards, though it covers four or five years, the action is more or less continuous. Although almost a year elapses in the chapter where Henchard is courting Susan and Farfrae is establishing himself as manager, and another year while Henchard is living with Elizabeth-Jane above the shop where he has been set up as a retailer of seeds, both of these episodes are economically presented, and there is little slackening of the narrative drive.

After the gap of eighteen years, we are reintroduced to Henchard through the eyes of Susan and Elizabeth-Jane, who are watching him through the window of the 'King's Arms'. Though we do not yet know it, this episode shows Henchard at the crest of his fortunes; his decline starts even as he appoints Farfrae to be his manager since it already appears that Farfrae is more able than he. Hardy tells us that the sudden decline of Henchard starts with the scene of the furmity woman in court, but in reality it has started well before that. The sarcastic commentary of Henchard's fellow-diners at the 'King's Arms' and the question about the bad bread that is thrown at him show a community riddled with envy and malice towards all those who have suc-ceeded, all too ready to exult in any discomfiture; and particularly ready to exult in Henchard's at this juncture, and later when the entertainment is rained off and it is evident that Farfrae is becoming more popular than he.

The story of the Mayor moves sometimes straightforwardly, and sometimes in spurts. When the focus moves to Lucetta or to Mixen Lane the story of Henchard remains relatively static, but in propelling it forwards, even Hardy acknowledged that coincidence plays a considerable part. Reference has already been made to this but in the direct structure of the story the average reader cannot but feel that Newson's three separate arrivals in Casterbridge fit a little uneasily.

Hardy employs well-worn narrative devices as part of his structure: one might enumerate the use of letters to give a sudden twist to the plot, and an extensive use of overheard conversations. Equally there is much use of presenting events in a pattern: Henchard arrives at Casterbridge penniless and carrying the tools of his trade near the start, and leaves the town clad in just the same way near the end. The qualities of character that make him mayor cause his downfall – energy, determination and impulsive action. Farfrae takes over Henchard's business, his house, his wife-to-be, his position in the town, his step-daughter. When Susan and Henchard remarry, each is carrying a secret: his is Lucetta and hers is Elizabeth-Jane's true identity; and both of them have a secret from Elizabeth-Jane. Farfrae is presented throughout as a contrast to Henchard, as in a different way is Elizabeth-Jane.

There is also a considered use of contrast as part of the structure, particularly the juxtaposition of the serious and the comic: of Susan's last wishes and Christopher Coney's amusing but macabre reaction to them; the anger of the magistrates after the skimmity-ride; the quick disappearance of all the persons concerned, together with their instruments. The tired mood of the opening pages, with their tone of futility and disillusionment that is reflected in the vegetation as much as it is in the conversation, also forecasts the mood of much of the novel.

The overall structure, then, is much more carefully balanced than a casual reading of the novel might lead one to think. Some of the items referred to above are no doubt the instinctive style of a born storyteller with a sense for the dramatic but the overall control of pace and atmosphere is evident and impressive.

Themes

Few novelists select a theme and then write their story around it. The more common method is to exploit a literary success if one is fortunate enough to have one by following it up with something that is broadly similar. So it was with Hardy. The environment in which he grew up was to be his lasting inspiration and to provide the raw material for all of his great novels; and as his cousin was to say long afterwards, he wrote about real people. If then High-Place Hall is moved four hundred metres, most of the characters in *The Mayor of Casterbridge* were living people, though their appearance in the novel will often differ considerably from those on whom they are modelled.

The centre of the *Mayor* is its main character Michael Henchard and the contradictory passions that make up his personality. Apart from this, a number of ideas run through the novel, and perhaps the most obvious of these is the idea of Fate. Is there a malevolent force at work which affects human destiny and in particular frustrates all of Henchard's endeavours, or is it his wrong-headed behaviour that causes the disasters? There is some evidence for both points of view, the more so as this is a feature of a succession of Hardy's novels.

For the first view, one thinks of the astonishing number of coincidences in the story. A sailor comes into the tent where the auction is being held right at the crucial moment. Farfrae happens to stay in the next room to Susan at the 'Three Mariners' so that she can hear her husband through the thin partition. The weather conspires to ruin Henchard's entertainment by starting to rain just as it is beginning. Henchard finds out that Elizabeth-Jane is not his daughter on the same evening he has told her that she is; she believes him and intends to call him 'father'. Henchard asks Elizabeth-Jane to change her mind and go on living with him – just ten minutes too late. Farfrae wins Lucetta's heart three minutes before Henchard pays her a visit. (And these are but a few of the total number of coincidences.)

Yet for the great majority of these happenings the coincidence itself is less important than the aspects of character that allow events to develop as they do. In the examples above, the important aspect is that Henchard should ever have let his relationship with his wife get to the stage where he would consider acting as he does. His entertainment was conceived as a slightly vindictive way of outdoing Farfrae; he finds out that Elizabeth-Jane is not his daughter because he has deliberately disobeyed Susan's wishes; he has driven Elizabeth-Jane to accept Lucetta's offer through his coldness to her when he discovers she is not his daughter; and his visit to Lucetta has been purposely delayed through his own wounded pride.

The view of human nature that prevails throughout the book is more often than not pessimistic. Henchard's faults are all too obvious; but Farfrae seems distinctly cold beside him and wholly lacking in sensitivity in what appears the single-mindedness with which he takes over every aspect of Henchard's former position. Lucetta seems always ready to sacrifice any moral principles for the gratification of her own immediate wishes; Susan seems lacking in any fibre when she meekly allows Henchard to sell her. And if a sense of primitive justice motivates the residents of Mixen Lane, it is often confused with feelings of self-interest. Only Elizabeth-Jane emerges with an unblemished character, and the book closes with even her reproaching herself for not having searched Henchard out sooner, and feeling that happiness is 'but the occasional episode in a general drama of pain'.

It is possible to find other themes that Hardy, probably unconsciously, incorporated into his story. One of these is his own comment on what was the prevailing belief of his time – and one that resurfaces from time to time throughout English history – that any man can better himself through hard work. This is no doubt true of a very small number who have risen from nothing to become millionaires, but it is an impossibility for more than a very few. Henchard starts the novel as an expert hay-trusser, having risen above the status of a labourer, anxious to do well, and seeing his wife and child as a brake on his progress. The sale of his wife removes that brake – at huge cost to him as a person – and his energies bring about his rise until he is Mayor of Casterbridge. His fall is more rapid than his rise, and leads the reader to think about the vanity of human wishes when a self-made man, as inadequate as he is, comes so spectacularly to grief. It also serves as Hardy's comment on the ethos of his own time.

Chapter summaries, critical comment, textual notes and revision questions

Chapter 1

An out-of-work hay-trusser, his wife and little child are approaching the village of Weydon-Priors one evening in late summer after a hard day's walking. They do not speak to each other at all. When they reach the village they find that it is the day of the fair, and though most of the activity of the day is ended, some tents are still selling refreshments. Among these is one selling furmity, and the woman persuades her husband to enter this one in preference to one selling beer and cider; she realizes her mistake when the woman who sells the furmity shows herself ready to fortify the mixture with rum, and her husband is soon befuddled with it. He becomes more and more argumentative and aggressive, and decides to put his wife up for auction. Though initially nobody makes a bid, the man keeps increasing his asking price; suddenly a sailor who has just entered offers five guineas for the wife and child and takes them away with him. The woman throws her wedding ring across the tent at her husband as she leaves, the crowd gradually disperses and the hay-trusser is left snoring where he sits.

Commentary

The first sentence tells us that the novel is set about 1830, over fifty years before Hardy wrote it. At first the story moves slowly and there is a good deal of description which shows close observation of the way country people dress and behave. The hay-trusser is dressed in a way that indicates he is a skilled man; but we do not find out his full name until the end of the second chapter. He is to be the dominating character of the book, and from the start he is shown to be morose and moody in that he hardly acknowledges his wife's presence. The relationship of the two is thus shown, even at this early stage, to be the important feature; Hardy calls it 'stale familiarity', which is carried like 'a nimbus'. Michael Henchard then scarcely appears in a favourable light, and his relationship with his wife is reflected in the description of the countryside through which they walk: the very leaves are 'doomed' and the road is covered in dust which muffles their footsteps. There is a constant air of pessimism for not only does love seem to have disappeared from the relationship but work is scarce; cottages are being pulled down and their inhabitants left homeless. The conversation with the turnip-hoer makes the whole scene suddenly real and is an early example of Hardy's great strength – the realistic description of a countryman expressed through direct speech. The turnip-hoer is a realist in that he asks immediately why a hay-trusser is looking for work in autumn when all the hay has long since been put into hayricks. In a fine piece of irony Susan edges her husband towards the furmity tent, thinking to avoid the dangers of alcohol, only to find it is the theatre of the disaster that sets the novel on its course.

When the scene reaches the interior of the tent the speed of the action suddenly increases, and Hardy shows his sense of the dramatic by greatly increasing the amount of dialogue. The shock of the events is such that by the end of the chapter the reader is immersed in the story.

fustian A coarse-textured cotton cloth.

tanned i.e. leather.

breves A musical note of considerable length (as opposed to quavers which are short).

hay-trussing Cutting hay and fastening it into convenient bundles.

journeymen Workmen. Literally, those hired out by the day (Fr. *journée*).

furlough Leave.

thimble-riggers Conjurers.

readers of Fate Fortune-tellers.

Furmity A country drink made from wheat grain raisins and spices boiled in milk.

Sold Hear Indicates the vendor's lack of education.

maelstrom A celebrated whirlpool off the coast of Norway – here indicating that the wife had no control over the course events were taking.

staylace The laces for tightening up corsets.

'vation i.e. salvation.

guinea One pound and one shilling; now £1.05.

'od A contraction of 'God', and in country lore a way of avoiding blasphemy.

keacorn Throat.

the great trumpet The Day of the Last Judgment.

the maid His little daughter, Elizabeth-Jane.

Chapter 2

The next morning the young man awakes to find himself still in the furmity tent, with a hazy memory of the events of the day before that is jolted into realization of what had happened by the discovery of his wife's wedding ring on the ground. He walks away from the fairground wondering how he can find his wife and daughter, and in the first village he comes to enters the church. He swears an oath to God (only here does the reader find out his full name – Michael Henchard), and vows to avoid all strong liquors for the space of twenty-one years. He searches long and in vain; at length at a seaport he learns that people answering the description he has given have recently emigrated. Giving up the search he goes straight to the Wessex town of Casterbridge.

Commentary

Most of this chapter is devoted to carrying forward the story as rapidly as possible, but from the start the mood is notably more optimistic. The morning is sunny; the fly buzzing in the tent helps to give the scene its realism, and as Henchard emerges from the tent the atmosphere is crisper than it was in Chapter 1, the colours brighter and the shadows more distinct. Henchard appears in a slightly more attractive light than before. He is ready to confess that he has done his wife a great wrong but is equally ready to say that what has happened is partly her fault. Hardy describes his oath as 'fetichistic' and this is to be the first example of many others that occur during the course of the novel. In a chapter where he is the only character it is significant that Hardy returns to direct speech for his dramatic effect – though here of course it is a monologue. The chapter ends with Henchard's arrival at Casterbridge, preparing the reader for the leap forward in time that occurs in the next chapter and indicating that the first two chapters are in effect a prologue to the rest of the novel.

the Seven Sleepers had a dog This refers to seven young men of Ephesus who sought refuge from persecution in a cave and slept there

for 300 years, according to legend. Their dog accompanied them.
fetichistic Something involving ritual.
sacrarium The part of a church immediately in front of the altar.
foot-pace The place where the priest stands during communion.
clamped book Old Bibles often had brass clamps to keep them closed.

Chapter 3

Eighteen years have passed and two women now approach the village at Weydon-Priors: the woman of Chapter 1 and her grown-up daughter. The fair has changed; it is now poorer and smaller but although her circumstances are much reduced the furmity woman is still there. The former Susan Henchard now calls herself Mrs Newson; she and her daughter are in mourning for Richard Newson, whom they believe has been lost at sea. The furmity woman is able to tell them that Michael Henchard had given her instructions to direct them, should they come to enquire for him, to Casterbridge. Susan decides that she will follow him there.

Commentary

While there is a certain irony in the close correlation of the events of this chapter with the opening one, there is strong emphasis on the effects of time. It has aged Susan and brought Elizabeth-Jane to full bloom but the fair has declined greatly as nearby towns have taken on many of its former functions. The reduction in scale of the furmity woman's activities is close to being comic; the distaste shown by both Susan and Elizabeth-Jane (though for very different reasons) effectively stops this from being more than sardonically humorous. Hardy returns to direct speech for the confrontation with the furmity woman, allowing her to talk of the better times she has had and to repeat certain of her routines; equally the relationship between Susan and Elizabeth-Jane is expressed in conversation, while quietly conveying the important news that they believe Newson to be dead.

A glance . . . continuity This paragraph is strong in dramatic irony. The reader does not yet know that Elizabeth-Jane is not the Elizabeth-Jane of the first chapter, and does not discover this until Chapter 19. If he does know it, there are three distinct levels of meaning in Hardy's comment.

withy i.e. willow.
highfliers Swings set in a frame.
soi-disant Self-styled, so-called.

Chapter 4

Hardy uses a flashback to fill in the story of the years we know nothing about. Susan had lived with Newson in Canada and in Cornwall, not doubting the legality of the transaction by which she had become his 'wife'. Doubt is sown in her mind by a friend; soon afterwards Newson is apparently lost at sea. Susan therefore resolves to find her real husband and eventually arrives at Casterbridge, where she finds the people complaining about the poor quality of the bread.

Commentary

The reader learns a good deal about Susan's gentleness and naivety, and is prepared for the strenuous efforts to better herself that Elizabeth-Jane is to make later in the novel. She is anxious for deeper learning rather than social advancement; this would specially single her out for the approval of the majority of the Victorian reading public. The main purpose of the chapter is, however, to introduce us to Casterbridge, the town that is the stage for the novel and which Hardy here lovingly recreates as it looked when he was a boy. Its salient features appear immediately: the tree-lined avenues that radiate from Casterbridge; the vestiges of the Roman garrison town that are still visible; above all the town's direct reliance upon agriculture. There is, too, evidence of Hardy's deep interest in architecture and further examples of his reliance on local dialect in conversation when he wishes to convey atmosphere.

carking Distressing, harassing.
glazings Glass.
her mother's health . . . once had been Susan dies quite early in the
  story, and this is the first indication that her health is not good – a
  timely forecast since her death occurs when she is not much more than
  forty.
coomb Hollow.
champaign Open, level country.
brick-nogging Bricks laid in patterns to fill the space between timber
  framing of a house.

bill hooks Tools for cutting hedges.
mattocks Tools for loosening hard ground.
butter-firkins Measures for 25.5kg of butter.
seed lips Baskets from which seed was scattered.
pattens Shoes with wooden soles.
a grizzled church A good instance of Hardy's ability to combine
  closeness of observation with the description of features that measure
  out the life of the town.
case clocks Clocks in wooden cases (e.g. grandfather clocks).
Sicilian Mariners' Hymn A well-known hymn tune played by the
  church bells.
manna-food Food miraculously supplied to the Israelites on their
  journey through the Wilderness. (Exodus 16, 14–15).
swipes Thin beer.
growed wheat Wheat largly useless for baking because the embryo has
  just started to grow and has absorbed some of the nutriment that helps
  it to do so. This happens when the grain is too wet; it is largely invisible
  to the untrained eye.
plim Swell.

Chapter 5

Susan and Elizabeth-Jane are attracted by the sound of music to
the 'King's Arms', the most important hotel in Casterbridge,
where a 'great public dinner' is in progress. A flight of steps
opposite allows them to look into the room where the dinner is
taking place. Susan is discomfited to find that her husband is the
Mayor, obviously a man of power and position. She and her
daughter notice that while the wine is flowing freely, Henchard's
glass is filled with water; some local people tell them of Henchard's vow. He is clearly being criticized for the state of the
wheat he has sold recently.

Commentary

The scene in the 'King's Arms' is presented to us by one of
Hardy's favourite techniques in *The Mayor of Casterbridge* – that
of framing it through a window. He presents the scene initially
through the eyes of Solomon Longways, a member of his rustic
chorus; and the reader needs to be more than usually credulous
to think anyone could see so much detail from a flight of steps at
the other side of the street. Susan is clearly shocked by the
change that has overcome her husband; she feels faint at the

prospect of seeing him again but he is still the same man (with his dark 'temper under the thin bland surface') whom we met earlier. This is reflected too in the attitude to him of his employees which seems to be one of respect for his strength of character but which also shows the universal readiness to criticize someone in authority if anything can be laid against him. The point of view of the writer changes as the story progresses – at the start it is that of an outsider, but as the narrative continues it moves to the room where the banquet is being held and focuses on the Mayor himself. He seems a man without friends: his laugh is aggressive and nervous and he feels under attack from his fellows. To an attentive reader Henchard is less confident than he may appear.

fall Veil. Ladies wore veils attached to their hats which they pulled down over their faces when out walking. Modesty demanded that they should not show their faces.

akin to a coach i.e. related to a man wealthy enough to own a coach.

like sows nuzzling for acorns A touch of gentle satire at the expense of civic dignity.

rummers Large glasses.

Solomon Longways, Christopher Coney Two rustics whom Hardy uses as a chorus are here introduced by name.

Another two years Another hint that Elizabeth-Jane is not Henchard's daughter.

as the Lord . . . Jews Referring to the event in Exodus 32, 15–19 where the Israelites worship a golden calf.

to-year This year.

list A layer of unrisen dough resulting in a leathery base to the loaf.

Chapter 6

A young man of 'remarkably pleasant aspect' joins the group outside the window. When he hears Henchard say that the wheat cannot be reclaimed he sends him a note; as the diners sink into somnolence Henchard seeks out the young man who, he finds, has obtained lodgings at the 'Three Mariners'. Susan and Elizabeth-Jane have followed the young man's example, as the inn seems a respectable if modest one.

Commentary

This is our introduction to the character who is to have most influence on Henchard, Donald Farfrae. It is clearly a matter of luck that he has been in the right place at the right time, but there is an immediate contrast between the two men, the one light where the other is dark. The tension suddenly increases as his note is delivered to and read by Henchard; and the restless brooding and pacing about which characterize the Mayor is an indication of the importance of this tension in the story. The contrast with the town council quietly subsiding into the stupor of having eaten and drunk too well is notable. Hardy also uses the opportunity lovingly to recreate the inn that he had known in his youth, but which, by the time he wrote the novel, had been demolished.

yard of clay A long clay pipe.
four-centred Tudor arch The broad arch developed in England during the fifteenth century.

Chapter 7

The two women find that their room adjoins that of the young Scot, and that they can hear everything that goes on there. Elizabeth-Jane arrives with the meal that she has earned while working for the innkeeper, to find Susan listening to Henchard who has paid Farfrae a visit and is talking to him about his ideas for partially reclaiming the ruined corn. Henchard insistently offers him the post of his corn manager, but Farfrae firmly refuses as he has made up his mind to go to America; he also refuses to accept Henchard's offer of hospitality.

Commentary

An element that starts to become increasingly apparent is that of coincidence. It is chance that gives Susan and Elizabeth-Jane a room adjoining Farfrae's, enabling them to hear him talking to Henchard; there is dramatic irony in the fact that Henchard hints at a dark event in his past, unaware that Susan is listening. Perhaps most of all there is the irony that Henchard actively encourages the man to work for him who more than any other is to be the cause of his downfall. The close description of Farfrae is important in that it further emphasizes the contrast between him and Henchard; it gives the reason that Farfrae somewhat resembles Henchard's dead brother as the starting-point for the development of Henchard's attraction to him. Hardy uses the opportunity of describing further the nooks and crannies of the 'Three Mariners' with all their idiosyncrasies and inconveniences.

twelve bushel strength Refers to the amount of barley used to make a measure of ale. The inn brewed strong beer.

a quag A quagmire.

I am bad at science For Henchard his own lack of education is a huge drawback; here 'science' means any sort of abstract knowledge.

the dog days The hottest days of the year (3 July–11 August) when Sirius, the dog star, rises and sets with the sun.

to the pitching To the dregs.

Chapter 8

The scene moves to the assembled company in the 'Three Mariners' where Farfrae has gone and had been followed by Elizabeth-Jane. With his good manners, his stylish singing and the unusual nature of his background, he makes a deep impression on everyone there. Elizabeth-Jane particularly feels a deep affinity with him and his outlook on life.

Commentary

This chapter is principally devoted to the impact that Farfrae has on the people of Casterbridge. To them he is exotic, coming as he does from a part of the country that to them is utterly remote and likely to be filled with eternal snow and wolves. The main device used by Hardy is his ability to sing, as it is this that so affects the inmates of the 'Three Mariners' and is to be one of the things that deeply affect Henchard. Farfrae, in telling them they are mistaken, seems to show little sense of humour in that he is unable to distinguish a flippant remark from a serious one. We gain our first hint that really there is little sentiment about the man; he has no desire to return to the country that is the theme of his song, which is something Christopher Coney immediately recognizes. Everyone else seems ready to bask in Farfrae's charisma, including Henchard who is walking up and down outside.

dying fall A sound gradually dying away (*Twelfth Night* 1.1.4).
lammigers Lame folk.
cust Cursed.
rebelled . . . Gallows Hill History is a confused mess to Buzzford, who
   is referring to legends about the Civil War (1640-49) and the
   Monmouth Rebellion (1685) when Judge Jeffreys sentenced 300 to
   death for their part in it.
bruckle Rough and untrustworthy.
ballet i.e. ballad.
chine The rim of a barrel.
gaberlunzie Strolling beggar.
netting fish seines Mending fishing-nets.
staddles Supports for the floor with wide tops to discourage rats.
Flemish ladders Ladders that narrow slightly towards the top.

Chapter 9

Next morning after some deliberation Elizabeth-Jane's mother
sends her with a note to Mr Henchard. When she opens the
door to his office, Elizabeth-Jane is surprised to see Farfrae
there; he has changed his mind about going to America and
has decided to become Henchard's manager.

Commentary

Much of this chapter is occupied by a description of Casterbridge on a typical working day in autumn. It expands the
introductory material of Chapter 4 and gives glimpses of the
blaze of colour in the citizens' back gardens before it deals with
the farmers and vendors and their customers on a market day.
Functionally this gives time for Elizabeth-Jane to explore the
town, as well as allowing Henchard successfully to persuade
Farfrae to change his mind and start work in the office where we
meet him before the chapter ends. Henchard's business is shown
to be thriving, from the number of waggons that bear his name
and the whirl of activity to the rear of his house; we also gain
another glimpse of his compulsive generosity to one who is, after
all, a complete stranger. Henchard has already told Farfrae that
he is a 'rule o' thumb sort of man' and the contrast between the
two is developed further when he offers him two breakfasts.
There is distinct dramatic irony when we hear that the Scotch-
man spoke 'like a man who permanently ruled there'.

bloody warriors Wallflowers.
'chassez-déchassez' The name of a French dance with a to-and-fro movement right and left.
Terpsichorean figures Steps in dancing. Terpsichore was one of the Nine Muses of Ancient Greece and was patroness of the dance.
Cranstoun's Goblin Page A dwarf who plays practical jokes in Sir Walter Scott's *Lay of the Last Minstrel* (1805).

Chapter 10

Elizabeth-Jane is received in kindly fashion by Mr Henchard and he writes a note to her mother arranging to meet her that night. He encloses five guineas in the envelope.

Commentary

Before Elizabeth-Jane can speak to Henchard, Jopp arrives to obtain the job that he has considered as good as his. The appointment of Farfrae to this post is completely unknown to Jopp and is a bitter disappointment; and it tells us a good deal about Henchard. Human relationships are not his strong point, and his treatment of Jopp is peremptory and unfair. It contrasts greatly with his treatment of Elizabeth-Jane, which is kindly and considerate. His sending the exact sum that he had received for her is a signal to Susan that he is buying her back and wishes to make amends for his treatment of her; but it is also another example of the ritualistic streak that is so much a feature of his character.

like the quicker cripple at Bethesda He was always the one to be healed (See John, 5, 2–7).
rouge et noir (Fr.) red and black. The furnishings of Henchard's house indicate his wealth and to some degree his piety.
The Ring Maumbury Rings, Dorchester, is on the edge of the town on the Weymouth road; it was originally a Roman amphitheatre and has high banks that effectively conceal anyone inside.

Chapter 11

Hardy spends as much time setting the scene for the encounter between Susan and Michael Henchard as he does on the encounter itself. They meet as arranged and Henchard, while making it clear that he wishes to revive their marriage, is only too conscious of his position in the town and therefore of the need to avoid scandal. He therefore suggests that she should stay in the town and that he should court and marry her. He is most anxious that Elizabeth-Jane should not find out the truth.

Commentary

The lengthy historical introduction serves first to give a sombre tone to the encounter, which in any case takes place at dusk. It indicates that the events of the story are by no means the most melodramatic in a long procession of events that have taken place within the confines of the Ring. Its 'dismal privacy' fits well with the tone of the meeting and is another example of the series of settings that have qualities similar to the events Hardy describes. It would perhaps have been easier to treat the actual encounter as melodrama but Hardy deliberately avoids this by getting both Michael and Susan to hint at the inadequacies in their characters rather than letting them express vain regrets. As with most moments of high tension Hardy turns to dialogue; Henchard shows his lack of security by being over-sensitive lest anyone should see their meeting and by his concern lest his position as a man of power and influence should in any way be compromised.

Jötuns Giants of Scandinavian mythology.
Coliseum The ruined amphitheatre at Rome once used for the same purpose as this at Casterbridge.
the sanguinary nature of the games Gladiatorial displays frequently ended in actual death for participants.
Aeolian Aeolus was king of the winds; the Aeolian mode is one of the modes of medieval music.
rub Obstruction, difficulty; a metaphor from the game of bowls.

Chapter 12

Henchard finds Farfrae at work in the office when he returns home. He insists that Farfrae join him for supper and there he tells him the whole of the story that we know already. Henchard also reveals that he had promised to marry the young woman whom we later know as Lucetta Templeman. She had nursed him back to health after he had been ill when on a visit to Jersey. Deciding that this first responsibility is to Susan he asks Farfrae to draft a letter for him and encloses a cheque with it as some compensation.

Commentary

That Henchard should open his heart so completely to one whom he had known for only one day can only be called astonishing, particularly when he has previously spoken so little about his private life. It is a measure of the impulsiveness of his nature here finding expression in a different direction; also of his craving for affection when he feels he has met a kindred spirit. Henchard's open confession appears attractive and it is vital that he should win the reader's sympathy before he suffers the misfortunes that afflict him later in the novel. The chapter is almost entirely written in direct speech and is at its most effective when Henchard is describing depressions the like of which Farfrae has never known. Henchard therefore appears to be a man of integrity, and his humility is a quality that prepares him for tragic stature.

Achilles A Greek hero who was educated to be a hunter and a fighter rather than a scholar.
espaliers Trees trained to grow sideways, along a wall.
Laocoöns   In Greek mythology Laocoon was crushed to death with his two sons by two gigantic serpents.
like Job . . . birth 'Let the day perish wherein I was born' (Job, 3, 3). This reveals the morose, dark side of Henchard which we have seen already and which is such a feature of the book.

Chapter 13

Henchard arranges a cottage for Susan, courts her and, after two months, marries her.

Commentary

Henchard suffers a change of character as far as the townspeople of Casterbridge are concerned and it is clear that they find the contrast between the 'masterful coercive Mayor' and the 'poor fragile' Mrs Newson so ludicrous as to be funny. Hardy speaks of Henchard as being 'red and black', and his face 'darkens' whenever he hears Susan being spoken of disrespectfully. The Mayor's humourless quality is one of the few character traits he shares with Farfrae; once the wedding takes place, to the accompaniment of a wet November day, Hardy hands over the commentary to his rustic chorus. They provide those touches of humour that are signally lacking elsewhere, and they show in addition common sense, a delightful lack of self-consciousness and an originality in imagery.

town walls . . . tumuli . . . forts The past is rarely far from Hardy's narrative.
twanking Complaining.
jumps or night-rail Stays or night-dress.

Revision questions on Chapters 1–13

1 How does Hardy build up tension in the first two chapters?

2 Is there any method in the way Hardy describes the scenery in Chapters 1 and 2?

3 To what extent is Hardy's treatment of the minor characters in the first eight chapters satirical?

4 Give a full account of Henchard in the days of his prosperity. Are there any hints that he may be vulnerable?

5 Compare the presentation of Farfrae and Henchard as young penniless adventurers.

6 How does Hardy use the scene in the bar of the 'Three Mariners'?

7 What impression do we get of Elizabeth-Jane in this section?

8 What aspects of Casterbridge does Hardy choose to reveal in this section, and how do they help the narrative?

Chapter 14

As Susan and Elizabeth-Jane settle down into an affluence they have never before known, Elizabeth-Jane is able to withstand the temptation to live ostentatiously, fearing that Fortune may as easily take away as give. Susan shows disquiet when Henchard proposes that Elizabeth-Jane change her name from Newson to Henchard, and Elizabeth-Jane too shows that she dislikes the idea. A trick is played on Elizabeth-Jane and on Farfrae by a person unknown (but later revealed to have been Susan) who arranges that they should meet in a secluded spot.

Commentary

The action of this chapter is clearly intended to cover a considerable space of time. It shows Elizabeth-Jane reacting in a most balanced way to her new situation; wealth has in no way turned her head and she continues to dress soberly. She shows instinctive good taste and an interest in improving her mind, but most of all she is continually aware of the changes of fortune, and is ready to accept what fortune decrees. In all this she is in extreme contrast to her stepfather who at all times is dangerously impulsive, and whose relationship with his newly appointed manager seems to be becoming too intense for comfort. There is another strong hint to the alert reader from Susan that Elizabeth-Jane is not Henchard's daughter. The scene then moves to Durnover and to the practical joke played on Farfrae and Elizabeth-Jane in the hope of starting off a romance. We do not find out for another four chapters that Susan has been the author of the anonymous messages, and the withholding of this information is one of several times in the course of the novel that Hardy uses this technique. Farfrae's reaction towards Elizabeth-Jane seems to be that of the perfect gentleman.

Martinmas summer A late summer (the feast of St Martin is on 11 November).
Georgian The house had been built during the eighteenth century, when three successive King Georges were on the throne (George I, reigned 1714–27, George II, 1727–60, George III, 1760–1820).
coulter The iron cutter in front of the ploughshare.
spencer A close-fitting bodice.
at executions Hardy had seen one himself in this spot when he was young, and he never forgot it.
an eastern purlieu called Durnover The suburb's real name is Fordington, and Hardy's portrait of it is a vivid period-piece.
victorine A garment of fur worn around the neck and shoulders.

Chapter 15

Further emphasis is placed on Elizabeth-Jane's deep humility, but the focus soon shifts to the relationship of Henchard and Farfrae, as the seeds of jealousy have started to grow within Henchard. The apparent reason for this is that Farfrae overrides Henchard's order to Abel Whittle to go to work without his breeches; the more deep-seated reason is that Farfrae is superior to Henchard in his handling of the business and more tactful in his handling of people. Inevitably this means that he is better liked.

Commentary

It is plain at the start of this chapter that the relationship between Elizabeth-Jane and Farfrae is starting to develop. Its development is to be arrested, however, by the strains that are thrown on the friendship of Henchard and Farfrae by the Abel Whittle affair. Henchard's problems, now as before, are caused by his impulsive and domineering nature. Farfrae, however, is no less determined and it is fitting that Hardy should use an image from nature to describe the difference between the two men: 'the seed that was to lift the foundation of this friendship'. The Abel Whittle episode is a good example of Hardy's sense of humour at its most typical — wry, and with a distinctly bitter flavour to it.

the prophet Baruch In the Apocrypha 'And taking gold, as it were for a virgin that loveth to go gay, they make crowns for the heads of their gods.'

Rochefoucauld His *maximes morales* (1665) assume that self-love is the prime motive of human conduct.

fretted my gizzard Worried.

moment-hand Minute hand, which on a pendulum clock twitches every time the pendulum moves.

scantling Scrap.

fairing Present.

diment Diamond.

man o'wax Handsome (as might be found in a waxwork).

Chapter 16

On a national holiday Farfrae arranges a simple entertainment, only to find Henchard organizing a rival attraction. Bad weather ensures that most of the town patronizes Farfrae, and Henchard's jealousy increases so much that he says openly that his employee's time as manager is coming to an end. Farfrae takes him at his word.

Commentary

As a result of the Whittle episode, the developing relationship between Henchard and Farfrae becomes by ordinary standards a more normal one; but for Henchard it marks a decidedly cooler attitude to the man who is steadily becoming his rival. It takes a long time for Casterbridge to decide on any formal recognition of the national holiday, and Farfrae's idea of organizing an entertainment therefore shows a proper sense of decorum in that as yet he is young and anxious not to cause any offence. Henchard's rival entertainment grows from jealousy of his new manager, and his anxiety to outdo him by paying for it all himself is all part of the same instinctive desire to show himself the master. At the same time it indicates that Henchard possesses a generosity of spirit that he retains throughout the book. A defect in his character is compounded by the bad luck of the inclement weather, and the reader starts to feel ever more strongly that fortune has conspired against him. His reaction, as ever is impulsive; Alderman Tubber's distinctly tactless comments prompt him to dismiss Farfrae but we feel that anyone in the same position would probably feel hurt and frustrated and might well react in the same way.

not forgetting his principles i.e. that there would be no alcoholic liquor.
Correggio A famous Italian artist (1494–1534) whose soft and delicate paintings appealed to Hardy.
stunpoll Blockhead.
by a lift By lifting them and guessing their weight.
by a chaw By a mouthful.
randy Merrymaking.
top sawyer When planks were being cut using a two-man saw, the man standing below had all the sawdust fall on him.

Chapter 17

Farfrae sets up on his own as a corn and hay merchant (not at first in opposition to Henchard). He does very well but Henchard construes this as an insult and asks both Elizabeth-Jane and Farfrae to have nothing further to do with each other.

Commentary

Henchard's treatment of Farfrae here seems set to strangle the relationship with Elizabeth-Jane in its infancy; particularly regrettable when Farfrae is starting to release her from her inhibitions. Farfrae's purchase of a small corn business is another example of his business acumen but also another in the succession of actions that can only antagonize Henchard. As such it has to be seen as either tactless or provocative. In his turn Henchard has always made as many wrong decisions as right ones; now his personal feelings lead him into a bitter feud that he cannot win. We sense that his support among the townspeople has been based on fear and respect for a man of evident strength rather than on love, and now the evidence grows that under any stress that support is likely to prove fickle.

dark dense old avenues These are still a feature of Dorchester, and are to be found on the main approaches to the town and on the roads that mark the line of the Roman Walls.

a varden A farthing.

sniff and snaff Consenting to his attentions.

modus vivendi (Lat.) way of living close to one another.

finesse Subtlety.

Jacob in Padan-Aram Jacob said he would work for Laban, his father-in-law, and receive in return the black lambs and the brindled and spotted goats. From that time Jacob's flock prospered. (See Genesis, 30, 25–43)

Novalis A German author (1772–1801).

Faust A figure who appears repeatedly in European literature as one who sold his soul to the devil. Hardy is probably referring to the character as developed by Goethe (1749–1832).

Bellerophon A legendary Greek hero who was falsely accused of seducing Proteus's wife and exiled to Lycia. There the King set him many trials which he performed successfully. He was 'hated of all the gods' and wandered the earth.

Chapter 18

Henchard receives a request from Lucetta Templeman to
return all her letters; she tells him that she will shortly be passing
through Casterbridge. She is not on the coach when it arrives
and Henchard returns home with the letters. Susan is very ill,
and shortly dies, but not before she has written a letter to her
husband with instructions that it is not to be opened until
Elizabeth-Jane's wedding day. The chapter closes with the
chorus of rustics commenting on and giving atmosphere to these
events.

Commentary

Several of the most important parts of this chapter are in the
form of letters. In this Hardy is taking over one of the convent-
ions of the 18th-century novel, which was sometimes written as a
collection of letters. Lucetta's letter to Henchard is a generous
one; it indicates that she is ready to acknowledge that he is acting
properly even though his action may cause her some difficulty.
Henchard is quite ready to return all her letters; his behaviour
indicates the strong strain of moral integrity that he possesses. It
is important at this time, when his decline is about to begin in
earnest, that the reader should have a high opinion of Henchard. Susan's decline and death occur very quickly, but not
before Hardy has been able to reveal the craft that has
attempted to bring Farfrae and Elizabeth-Jane together, and
given indications of future developments in the mysterious
letter. The really memorable part of the chapter is, however, the
conversation of the rustics after Susan's death. It has a macabre
quality that exactly reflects Hardy's own interests, and if Susan's
last requests (relayed at third hand) appear sentimental, one
does not know whether the emphasis comes from Susan, the
Nurse, Mother Cuxsom or from all three; and Christopher
Coney's immediate and practical use of her ounce-pennies is full
of wry amusement.

Antelope Hotel The Hotel stands in the little square named Cornhill in
the centre of Dorchester.
ounce pennies Heavier than normal pennies and minted for special
occasions.
doxology He means theology.

Chapter 19

All of Henchard's affections are directed towards Elizabeth-Jane
now that Susan is dead and Farfrae estranged. He decides to tell
her what he believes is the truth: that she is really his daughter;
he also persuades her to change her name to Henchard. Almost
immediately afterwards he comes across a letter written to him
by the dying Susan with instructions that it is not to be opened
until Elizabeth-Jane's wedding-day, and the seal she has put on it
has cracked. He cannot resist the temptation to read the letter
and he finds out from it that his own daughter had died, and
Elizabeth-Jane is Newson's, born a year after Henchard's separ-
ation from Susan. He decides not to tell Elizabeth-Jane this, but
feels that the essence has been subtly removed from their relationship.

Commentary

Of the many blows that fortune rains upon Henchard, this is one
of the cruellest, particularly in its timing; had he waited for just
one more day, he would not have suffered in the way he is made
to. By these means the reader's sympathy for him is steadily
increased. There follows the episode where he walks along the
riverbank on the north-eastern side of the town, one of the more
notable instances of Hardy's harmonizing his background with
the melancholy tone of Henchard's thoughts. The gothic para-
phernalia of gallows, gaol, hangman's cottage and the mention
of rheumatic disorders could easily become melodramatic,
which is only avoided by the closeness of Hardy's observation.

pier-glass A bevelled mirror hung between the windows.
entablature Another of Hardy's characteristic architectural terms.
like the brethren . . . Joseph Refers to the arrival of Joseph's brothers
  in Egypt where, after they had sold him into slavery, he had risen to
  high office; they were embarrassed on seeing him. (Genesis, 45, 1–3)
like a great tree in a wind A characterful and forceful image to
  describe Henchard at this juncture.
Prester John A mythical king who tried to spread his conquests to
  Paradise itself and was punished by the gods, who set a rich banquet
  before him and made harpies snatch the food away whenever he tried
  to eat, so that he starved to death.
Schwarzwasser Black water – the German name for a Polish river.

Chapter 20

Henchard increasingly finds fault with Elizabeth-Jane – in her speech, her manner and her lack of sophistication. His constant criticisms and coldness make her miserable. Deliverance comes from a lady she meets by her mother's grave, whom we later find out to be Lucetta; she has just bought a house in the town and she invites Elizabeth-Jane to be her housekeeper-companion.

Commentary

The tension steadily increases. Henchard's criticisms of Elizabeth-Jane are a direct result of his ungovernable passions, and all of them reflect a terrible insecurity. As Hardy comments on her quaint use of dialect, it is 'the mark of the beast to the truly genteel', but it is the actions which suggest that her social status is less than it now appears to be that deeply anger him. Her humility too is perhaps more irritating to him than outright opposition would have been. At this stage Lucetta is introduced but her name is deliberately withheld by Hardy in order to increase the mysterious element – this is another instance of a technique calculated to sell more copies of the next issue of *The Graphic*.

jowned Shaken up; the meaning is no more than 'indeed'.
Minerva The Roman name for Athena, goddess of wisdom and strength; here a woman with masculine characteristics.
bristling characters Handwriting with delicately formed letters.
the Princess Ida A character in Tennyson's *The Princess* (1847) who organizes a university for women.
chain-shot and sandbags i.e. writing that was much coarser.
Hadrian . . . the Constantines Roman Emperors; it was customary in Roman times to bury the dead with a coin in the mouth to pay the dead person's fare across the river Styx.
avenues of Karnac Either the avenues of monoliths at Carnac in Brittany or the ancient town of Thebes in Egypt.
Austerlitz A battle (1805) which marked the climax of Napoleon's military successes.
leery Exhausted.

Chapter 21

Elizabeth-Jane looks at High-Place Hall and obtains Henchard's permission to leave home; she decides to go immediately despite a last minute attempt to dissuade her.

Commentary

Hardy includes in this chapter several incidents calculated to arouse the reader's expectations while at the same time continuing the minute depiction of the features of Casterbridge. His point of view is constantly shifting; so we learn of Elizabeth-Jane's visit to and tentative exploration of High-Place Hall through her eyes, then as she hears someone coming along the alley behind the house and quickly conceals herself it is the omniscient novelist who tells us that the someone was Henchard. Henchard's coldness and apparent indifference towards her are balanced by his offer to pay her an annuity; it is characteristic of Hardy generally and of this novel in particular that his change of heart and appeal to her to change her mind and to continue to live with him come only minutes too late to make her change her mind.

Palladian A style of building in the manner of the Italian architect Palladio and introduced to England by Inigo Jones in the seventeenth century, when the classical style superseded the Gothic.
tailing The small bits of corn that get away from the main mass.
fly Small carriage.

Chapter 22

The story moves backwards to the night before when Elizabeth-Jane watched Henchard enter the High-Place Hall. We find that Lucetta has written to him telling of an abrupt change in her fortunes, that she has abandoned her previous name of Le Sueur and taken the name of her aunt, Templeman. Lucetta is unable to see him and he construes this as an insult. As a result, and through obstinacy, he fails to visit her for any of the next three days. Lucetta learns from Elizabeth-Jane that Henchard will not come because she is there. Lucetta's plan has failed; she had hoped that Henchard could visit her regularly under the pretence of visiting his own daughter, thereby allaying any local gossip. On the Tuesday morning Lucetta sends Elizabeth-Jane on an errand, while dispatching a note to Henchard telling him that his daughter will be out and that he need not fear meeting her. A visitor calls – but it is Farfrae, not Henchard.

Commentary

Letters are used three times in this chapter to carry the story forward. All are written by Lucetta and all reflect a strong element of indiscretion, which makes her anxiety to have her letters returned understandable. Her comment on Susan as being 'weak in intellect' but 'not an imbecile' also suggests that she is tactless. The element of chance again is very strong: one notices Lucetta's unwillingness to see Henchard when he calls; his sulky refusal to call again next day when he would have been more than welcome; and the chance arrival of Farfrae. Lucetta in her turn seems as impulsive as Henchard, distinctly given to striking dramatic poses for maximum effect when she 'arranged herself picturesquely in her chair'. Finally it is noticeable how the dramatic tension rises with the introduction of Farfrae, whether he is in the market-place or calling at High-Place Hall.

Mon ami (Fr.) my friend. Hardy emphasizes Lucetta's connection with the Channel Islands by giving her expressions such as this; French was the normal language of the Islands until relatively recent times.
étourderie (Fr.) thoughtlessness.
boudoir Lady's small private room.
Titian A famous Venetian painter (c.1490–1576) noted for his painting of scenes from classical mythology.
the weak Apostle St Peter, who was told that his accent gave him away (Matthew, 26, 73).
netting Ladies made netting as the ground material for fine embroidery.
carrefour (Fr.) crossroad.
Candlemas fair Originally a festival of the Catholic Church celebrated on 2 February and which continued, after the Reformation, to be used for various secular functions.
cyma-recta An architectural term meaning that her profile assumed a concave curve.

Revision questions on Chapters 14–22

1 How is the national holiday used to contrast Henchard and Farfrae?

2 Is our opinion of Farfrae anything other than favourable up to the end of Chapter 22?

3 To what extent in these chapters do characters really communicate with one another?

4 Contrast Henchard's treatment of Elizabeth-Jane when he thought she was his daughter with his treatment of her after he knew she was not.

5 How is Lucetta introduced into the story, and how is her character developed?

6 Compare the death of Susan with the way the Casterbridge residents react to it.

Chapter 23

Farfrae has called at High-Place House while searching for Elizabeth-Jane. Lucetta finds him stimulating company, and persuades him to wait. They talk about their various circumstances while watching the market in progress outside, and Farfrae wins Lucetta's active sympathy by deciding to employ a young man who, it appears, may be separated from his love and refuses to go anywhere without his old and nearly incapable father. Farfrae leaves to do business, and Lucetta is so impressed by him that when Henchard eventually arrives she declines to see him, pleading a headache.

Commentary

The Farfrae of this chapter is the same Farfrae who has appeared earlier in the novel, lithe, handsome and attractive in his ways. He is no sentimentalist who longs to get back to Scotland but a businessman who is doing well and is already a considerable rival to Henchard. The episode where he ensures that the two lovers will not be separated takes a considerable part of the narrative, and is one of the means by which he exerts a fascination on Lucetta even stronger than that which his qualities have already given him. The chapter is also strong in irony in that by arriving in order to see Elizabeth-Jane he is in fact led to think of her less, and in that he also serves to direct Lucetta's thoughts away from Henchard. The part played by chance continues to grow.

hyperborean Belonging to the extreme North.
kerseymere Cloth of fine wool.
St Helier The chief town on the island of Jersey.
hiring fair The fair when people wanting employment offered
  themselves for hire, each wearing the characteristic dress of his
  occupation.
wagon-tilts Canvas coverings of wagons.
Lady-day 25 March, a quarter-day named after the Annunciation to
  the Virgin Mary.
Cupid Son of Venus, the Roman goddess of love. 'Dan' is an
  abbreviation of the Latin 'dominus' meaning 'Master'.

Chapter 24

Lucetta and Elizabeth-Jane find that High-Place Hall is a good
vantage-point to observe all the activities of Casterbridge, and
they soon find themselves eagerly looking forward to market-
day. One Saturday the arrival of a new seed-drill gives an opportunity to meet first Henchard then Farfrae; Elizabeth-Jane sees
that Lucetta is considerably attracted by the young Scot. A few
days later Lucetta tells Elizabeth-Jane the story of her attraction
towards both men as if she is talking of a third person, but
Elizabeth-Jane guesses the truth.

Commentary

This chapter starts with the arrival of new dresses from London
for Lucetta; Casterbridge is too provincial to supply her with
suitable clothes. The scene in which, together with Elizabeth-
Jane, she looks at the two dresses is an example of Hardy's use of
incidents for their symbolic as much as for their functional
purpose. For Lucetta *is* the clothes she wears; striking in appearance but with very little behind the surface glamour. The way
she has spread them out on the bed indicates a desire to impress,
and it takes the supposedly inexperienced Elizabeth-Jane to see
that such an obsession is not worth the trouble it causes. Equally
symbolic is the new seed-drill. Henchard pours scorn on it,
though at least partly through jealousy; Farfrae, who has recom-
mended that it be bought, sees its uses and mentions that
machines such as this are already in widespread use elsewhere in
England. The drill thus reflects the difference between the two
men, and shows that Henchard belongs to the past, Farfrae to

the future. Lucetta's conversation with Elizabeth-Jane shows that she is used to a measure of duplicity and now uses it again, but she does not expect Elizabeth-Jane to show the insight that she does.

the Heptarchy Saxon England.
some falls by the wayside . . . some among thorns From the parable of the sower (Matthew, 13, 3–9).
'He that observeth . . . shall not sow' Also Biblical (Ecclesiastes, 11, 4).
rencounter Casual meeting; from the French *rencontre*.

Chapter 25

Elizabeth-Jane becomes a witness of, and a commentator upon, the arrivals at High-Place House of both Farfrae and Henchard as suitors for Lucetta; if Farfrae has the fervour of youth, it is Henchard who impresses us most with his genuine wish to make amends to her for the events of the past – only to be rejected. Elizabeth-Jane is quite forgotten, but shows herself 'Susan Henchard's daughter' in accepting the situation.

Commentary

Of the two suitors, the sympathy of the reader is directed mainly towards Henchard; despite his lack of polish, his ignorance of styles of furniture and his awareness that 'his accents and manner wore a roughness not observable in the street', he displays a genuineness of feeling that marks him as superior to the relatively anaemic Farfrae. Farfrae's indifference to the Elizabeth-Jane in whom he had shown such interest not long before can only be an indication of a certain shallowness of character. It is perhaps Elizabeth-Jane who most gains the reader's sympathy; she has been sought after in turn by Henchard, by Farfrae and by Lucetta and here she suffers the wounding experience of being ignored by all three. She emerges from the experience creditably enough to be an interesting contrast to Henchard, whose reactions to misfortune are so different.

Protean Readily assuming different shapes. Proteus was Neptune's herdsman and could change his shape at will.
'meaner beauties of the night' The stars, when measured against the power of the moon. The quotation is from Sir Henry Wotton's poem 'The Queen of Bohemia', written in the mid-seventeenth century.

Chapter 26

Henchard starts to suspect that Lucetta has conceived an interest in someone else, but he has no proof. While visiting her for tea he meets Farfrae there, and in the slightly uneasy time they spend together it becomes plain to Elizabeth-Jane that Lucetta is falling in love with the Scot. Henchard employs Jopp (the manager originally displaced by Farfrae) as his manager and gives him instructions to 'cut out' Farfrae by ruining him commercially; Jopp is more than ready to get his revenge on his rival. In pursuit of his objective Henchard visits the weather-prophet Fall, and hears that the weather in August is likely to be bad. He buys heavily in anticipation of this and when the weather is in fact good loses correspondingly. He dismisses Jopp and makes yet another enemy.

Commentary

The symbolic centre of this chapter is the struggle between Henchard and Farfrae for the slice of bread and butter at Lucetta's tea party. The mode of its presentation contains elements of comedy, for the contrast between a Tuscan painting on a biblical theme and the scene described by Hardy is so extreme as to be a comic comment on the persons involved. Henchard's visit to Fall is, in contrast, melodramatic, but a good example of the way in which Hardy works into his novels the atmosphere of the Dorset he had known as a boy; its presentation in dialogue increases the impression of melodrama. Above all we can see the rashness of Henchard in staking all his resources on so dubious a plan.

refluent Flowing back.
gazebo Another architectural term, meaning a summer-house built to command a view.
Tuscan painting A style which was a precursor of the Florentine painters of the fifteenth century and which was stiff by comparison with them.
the two disciples supping at Emmaus See Luke, 24, 13–35.
pis aller (Fr.) last resource.
scarecrow green i.e. faded green.
immediately before . . . trade in grain The Corn Laws, imposing a heavy duty on foreign corn, to protect the home farmer, were repealed by Sir Robert Peel in 1846.

Alastor An avenging god.

the bell-board A small table with bells arranged in order; each ringer controlled several bells and had to ring his particular bell at the right time to make a tune. The expression therefore means that the prosperity of Casterbridge depended on the surrounding villages.

water-tights Water-tight boots.

springes Snares.

he was sometimes astonished . . . believe so little A cynical comment which hints at the agnostic that Hardy had become.

like Saul . . . Samuel i.e. surprised and somewhat embarrassed (See 1 Samuel, 9, 1–24).

the evil Scrofula, a disease which enlarges the lymphatic glands, and was formerly thought to be curable by a touch from the King.

toad-bag A bag full of the legs torn from living toads; if worn round the neck these were supposed to be an excellent remedy for scrofula.

dung-mixen Dunghill.

living in Revelations When the four angels blew trumpets heralding the end of the world (Revelation, 8, 7–12).

like tin i.e. pale.

Chapter 27

Soon after the harvest starts the weather changes for the worse; the price of grain rises. Had Henchard delayed selling his corn he would not have lost a great deal, and he comes to believe that the fates are in league against him, as Farfrae quietly prospers. The rivalry between the two men is taken up by their employees, and Henchard attempts once more to see Lucetta, only to be told that she is committed to going out. He follows her and finds out that her assignation is with Farfrae; he hears some of their conversation. Returning to High-Place Hall he arrives there before Lucetta and enters her house. Before Elizabeth-Jane as a witness, he makes Lucetta promise to marry him under threat of revealing their intimacy. Elizabeth-Jane cannot understand the power that her father has over Lucetta.

Commentary

As usual, the reader has a mixture of feelings towards Henchard. His financial ruin is not completely his fault, and Lucetta is less than fair in her treatment of him. At the same time he supports his carter with scant evidence that he was in the right; no-one has much sympathy for those who eavesdrop intentionally, and his ideas on how to win Lucetta seem distinctly primitive. Hardy prepares for later developments in the story by reintroducing the furmity woman and showing Lucetta's fragility by her fainting; Stubberd's malapropisms are the start of a series of appearances where the town constable is made to seem ridiculous. The life of Casterbridge is further developed by the encounter of the two carts which gives a glimpse of the town in earlier days when baiting oxen with dogs was the usual practice before they were killed; and we see the frantic haste to bring in the harvest when the weather was threatening, which made the workers cut corn by moonlight.

conjuror In its sense of 'one who invokes devils'.
roasting . . . brew Both were regular practices of magic. Witches were supposed to make waxen images of people upon whom they wished to bring mischief, then stick pins in them or roast them.
confound In its old sense of 'ruin' or 'damn'.
Capitol The centre of administration in an important Roman town.
zwailing Swaying, wandering.
gawk-hammer Awkward, stupid.
thill One of the horses between the shafts.
giddying worm A parasite, which, if eaten by a sheep, will cause it to become giddy and eventually die.
flagrant A malapropism for 'vagrant'.
shocks Sheaves of corn that have been propped against each other at intervals throughout a field.
lucubrations Night studies.
no'thern Wandering (mentally), incoherent.

Chapter 28

Henchard in his capacity as a magistrate is in court next morning when the furmity-woman is brought before him. She reveals his past; admitting that what she says is true he leaves the court and refuses to judge her. Lucetta is deeply disturbed when she hears this story and leaves Casterbridge to spend a few days in Port-Bredy; Henchard calls to enquire after her on two occasions.

Commentary

The scene in the courtroom is one where Hardy shows his sense of humour, and as usually happens with him, that sense is sardonic and satirical. It appears in the furmity-woman's testimony, which shows her to be better versed in the procedure of a magistrate's court than the magistrates themselves; in Stubberd's comically delivered evidence; and in the difficulties of the clerk in writing it down. The text states that Henchard had no need to listen to the furmity-woman's accusation, and that he could have denied its truth without anyone disbelieving him. That he chooses to tell the truth is to his credit, though his sudden departure from the court increases the drama of the episode and inevitably hastens the decline in his reputation.

Petty Sessions Courts for the trial of minor offences by magistrates.
Shallow and Silence Country justices from Shakespeare's *Henry IV, Part 2*, who are shown to be incompetent and corrupt.
ashlar A building constructed of stone that has been cut to a regular shape.
clouds drop fatness From Psalm 65,11.
instinct, Hannah Dominy i.e. instant, anno domini – and therefore mild satire at the expense of the constable, who knew neither the correct form nor its meaning.
wambling Moving unsteadily, staggering.
turmit-head i.e. turnip-head or blockhead.
larry Commotion.

Chapter 29

Henchard saves Lucetta's life by rescuing her from a fierce bull. He asks her if she will intercede with his main creditor, a man named Grower, by hinting that they are engaged. Lucetta says that she cannot do this because she has just married Farfrae, and Grower was one of the witnesses. Henchard is devastated by the news.

Commentary

Henchard again appears attractively in this chapter; he is courteous and attentive as well as brave, and his generosity has made him reconsider the promise that he earlier wrung out of Lucetta. His request to her to help him out of his financial difficulties appears reasonable, and in refusing it Lucetta at first seems unreasonable – because Hardy purposely delays telling us about her marriage to Farfrae. The information is almost as much a surprise to us as it is to Henchard. It seems somewhat deceitful of Lucetta to have slipped off to get married at Port-Bredy, sixteen miles away; and to Henchard, any chance of happiness is receding because the woman he might have been happy with has been taken from him by the man he has most cause to dislike and fear.

with Abrahamic success See Genesis, 13,2.

Yahoo The name given by Swift in *Gulliver's Travels* (Book 4) to a class of animals that have the forms of men but the understanding and passions of the lowest brutes.

the Thames . . . yore The Thames Tunnel, opened in 1843, was the greatest engineering triumph of the early Victorian age. Toys were modelled on it.

Gurth's collar of brass Gurth, the faithful swineherd in Scott's *Ivanhoe* (1819) had a brass ring soldered fast around his neck.

a sirocco The name given in Italy to the dry south wind which has come from the Sahara.

Chapter 30

Farfrae prepares to move into High-Place Hall and Lucetta realizes that she has not yet told Elizabeth-Jane of the marriage. She tells her and is surprised by the violence of the young woman's reaction. Elizabeth-Jane has an inbuilt sense of propriety and feels that Lucetta has acted dishonourably; she decides immediately that she must move out, and takes lodgings in the street where Henchard lives.

Commentary

Farfrae realizes soon enough when he moves in to High-Place Hall that the situation is likely to prove embarrassing for Elizabeth-Jane. Lucetta does not know of their brief affair earlier in the story; she goes to tell Elizabeth-Jane confident that she will be able to reconcile her to the new development. Elizabeth-Jane at first seems excessively naive in that she does not know what everyone else seems to know; Hardy then emphasizes her intelligence in that, on very little evidence – on intuition rather – she guesses what has happened. Her guess that Lucetta has in fact married Henchard is calculated to make the situation as embarrassing as possible for Lucetta when she admits that she has in fact married Farfrae. Elizabeth-Jane's rigid moral principles give her character a positive side that up to now has not been much in evidence; her recommendation that Lucetta stay single and then her decision that she must immediately leave High-Place Hall would have appealed to the correct Victorian reader.

like John Gilpin From Cowper's well-known ballad poem of that name. John Gilpin got down from the horse he had just mounted, in order to attend to customers.

Ovid From his *Metamorphoses*. The quotation means: 'I see the better things and approve of them; I follow the worse.'

Nathan tones i.e. damning tones such as were used by the prophet Nathan in condemnation of David for his marriage to Bathsheba (2 Samuel, 12, 1–9).

seines Large fishing nets.

Chapter 31

Henchard's fortunes decline rapidly. His character is blackened by news of the wife-sale and his business falls off to such a degree that he is declared bankrupt. He wins the approval of his creditors for his honesty in dealing with them; but he leaves his house, goes into poor lodgings in Jopp's cottage, and gives orders that no one is to be admitted to see him. Even Elizabeth-Jane is unable to pay him a visit; she learns that Farfrae has bought Henchard's business and his house.

Commentary

As Henchard's fortunes decline our sympathy for him increases. This process is helped by a number of incidents: his decline into bankruptcy is only partly his own fault and has been compounded by the failure of another to whom he had lent money; the misguided energy of one of his employees who had removed faulty grain from a sample and thus misrepresented what the bulk had been like; his generosity in giving his last possession to his creditors, and particularly the watch which he sold to relieve the needs of a creditor who was himself in financial straits; and by the information given by Abel Whittle to Elizabeth-Jane when he tells her that the men now have to work harder for less pay. The business may be run more efficiently, but some of its soul has departed. Henchard's dejection that makes him look down-wards in the street, take lodgings in an obscure corner of the town and refuse to see any visitors, raises sympathy for him to the extent that his status is becoming that of a tragic hero.

the Commissioners Corresponding to the modern Receiver – the person appointed by the Court to administer the property of a bankrupt.

Boldwood, Everdene Names familiar as those of farmers who appear in *Far from the Madding Crowd* (1874).

vitrified With blue glazed bricks laid in a pattern with the brown ('dun') ones.

sash-bars The rectangular divisions that hold the panes of glass.

window-jambs Side pieces of window-frames.

arch-labels Mouldings over doors, windows etc., or parts of them.

cat-head A beam projecting from the wall and used to haul up sacks into a granary.

Chapter 32

On the eastern side of Casterbridge the main road crosses two bridges in succession. To them come all the failures of the town, and we see Henchard meeting first Jopp, who tells him that Farfrae has bought his house and furniture, then Farfrae, who offers him room to live in his old house. He has bought the furniture with the intention of giving it back to Henchard, who refuses the offer, and realizes that he may have wronged Far-frae. Henchard goes to live in a cottage, but falls ill and is confined to his room. Elizabeth-Jane hears of this and goes to see him once more; this time she will not be denied admission. Time passes and Henchard asks for work as a hay-trusser. He is taken on but is often morose and moody at the reversal of his fortunes. At the end of the chapter we hear that he has started drinking again.

Commentary

This chapter marks what is nearest to a moment of calm in the progress of the novel so far. This is reflected in the static but very atmospheric opening describing the two bridges from two distinct points of view. One of these is the architectural – the 'weather-stained brick' (that Hardy had crossed every day on his way to school for many years). The other is social, showing the bridges as a focus for the unsuccessful elements in Casterbridge society and which draw people to them by some secret magnetism. Henchard is shown here in a way that makes it seems possible he could regain some of his self-respect — only for that possibility to recede rapidly as he starts drinking again. Farfrae is presented at first as being tactless in the extreme as he is directly supplanting Henchard in so many ways; but he is then shown to have some magnanimity and generosity as he buys Henchard's furniture with the intention of giving it back to him, offers him accommodation in his house and immediately offers him employment when he seeks it.

Adonis A handsome youth of classical mythology loved by Venus, the goddess of love.
journey-work i.e. work as a hired day-labourer.
the Prophet's chamber The chamber of Elisha in Shunem (2 Kings, 4, 8–11).
stock A wide band serving the purpose of collar and tie.

Chapter 33

Henchard decides to celebrate the end of his twenty-one years of abstention in the 'Three Mariners' on a Sunday. The choir comes in from the church opposite and he insists that they sing for him the words of a psalm that have a savage bearing on the situation he is in. The singers and musicians dissociate themselves from its sentiments. It becomes clear to Elizabeth-Jane, who finds him there, that Farfrae may be in danger; she decides to keep a close eye on Henchard while he is in work.

Commentary

It is entirely typical of Hardy that he should select one of the bitterest parts of the Bible for the recital that Henchard sponsors. It gives an ominous twist to what might otherwise be an unexceptionable account of a Casterbridge Sunday, written at a time when the old disciplines meant that nearly everyone attended church, listened attentively to the sermon, and to music provided by a motley collection of instrumentalists; and retired afterwards to seek refreshment at the inn just across the road. It is clear that Henchard's bitterness alarms the company in the 'Three Mariners' as much as it alarms Elizabeth-Jane; and the same tone is conveyed by Henchard's scathing sarcasm when he talks to Lucetta in the hay-barn. Elizabeth-Jane's chance arrival, to see her stepfather threatening by his appearance to push Farfrae to his death, fills the reader with apprehension as to what will happen next.

the choir The service was accompanied by a group of instrumentalists usually seated in the west gallery of the church. Any who could play a musical instrument took part.
dramless i.e. without taking a dram of liquor.
Sound A i.e. tune your instruments.
stave Verse (of a hymn).
ballets Songs with a 'fa la la la la' refrain.
rantipole rubbish Wild and rough.
Wiltshire A hymn-tune still in use today.
Servant David David was long supposed to have written all the psalms.
'Mistress, know yourself . . .' From *As You Like It* (III, 5, 57–8).
trap Trapdoor.

Revision questions on Chapters 23-33

1 How close is the relationship of Lucetta and Farfrae?

2 In what way in this section is Lucetta confirmed as a coquette?

3 'In this section, Elizabeth-Jane seems increasingly colourless.' Do you agree?

4 This section starts with Henchard as Mayor and ends with his starting to drink again. How is such a sudden change made convincing?

5 How are the everyday activities of Casterbridge made into an effective part of the narrative?

6 Why is the episode of the bull included? What does it show us about relationships between the characters?

Chapter 34

Elizabeth-Jane, at much cost to herself, gives a vague warning to Farfrae. He makes light of it but the warning is not lost on him. He had planned to help Henchard by setting him up in a seedsman's shop, but is told by the town clerk that Henchard hates him, so gives up the idea. Henchard hears only that Farfrae has opposed the plan and this further fuels his enmity. On meeting Henchard in the market Lucetta again asks him to return her letters; he remembers that they are in his old safe at what is now Farfrae's house. He arranges to call for the letters, intending to read them out and at the end to tell Farfrae the name of the author. In the event he is unable to bring himself to do something that may wreck their marriage, and takes the letters quietly away.

Commentary

After the initial events, which remind us of the earnestness and worth of Elizabeth-Jane, the focus shifts to Farfrae; at first the quietly self-confident businessman, he is shown to be essentially kindly and charitable towards Henchard and an attentive and loving husband to Lucetta. At the same time his comments on Scotsmen who were 'not lucky' shows him to have a limited sense of humour, and his readiness to accept the offer of the mayoralty further emphasizes his lack of sensitivity. Henchard here appears totally exposing the two violently polarized elements in his personality. His plan to read out the letters publicly, before finally revealing to Farfrae his affair with Lucetta, reveals the worst side of his nature in its vindictiveness. The failure of his nerve which prevents him from doing so shows his more attractive side. Hardy builds up the dramatic tension to considerable effect in this last section, while Farfrae listens to the recital with a bored indifference that the reader knows could be transformed in a moment were the identity of the writer revealed.

siller shoon Scottish form of 'silver shoes'.
Tamerlane's trumpet The great Tartar conqueror (c. 1330–1400), who appears variously as Tamburlaine or Timur the Lame, was said to have used huge trumpets.
Aphrodite The Greek goddess of love.
subscription What was written underneath – the signature.

Chapter 35

Lucetta has overheard the events of the previous chapter, and this causes her dreadful anxiety and suspense. When Farfrae comes to bed she realizes that Henchard has not revealed their past relationship, and after a sleepless night she writes him a note asking him to meet her at dusk – at the Ring. For the meeting she wears dark clothes that lessen her natural attractions. Her demeanour and the fact that she has selected this scene, which reminds him powerfully of Susan, causes Henchard to promise that he will return the letters the next day.

Commentary

This chapter contains two highly dramatic, indeed melodramatic, episodes centred on Lucetta; in the first Henchard appears almost as a villain and in the second as very much more human in his response. The scene where Henchard reads out Lucetta's letters to Farfrae uses a technique characteristic of Hardy – the overheard conversation. He has used it before in Chapter 27 and it appears in other of his novels, notably in *Tess of the d'Urbervilles*. It increases the tension powerfully. The reader shares Lucetta's anxiety as to whether her secret will be kept and at the same time can see further, to the cause of her distress, which, we can see, is her insecurity and the volatile nature that makes her commit her thoughts to paper in a way that can only be called rash. Her reluctance to tell Farfrae of her past stems from a pathetic desire to keep him, and a fear that if she tells him she will lose him even now that they are married. The scene in the Ring is strongly reminiscent of Henchard's meeting with Susan at the same place and for that reason appeals to the fetichistic side of his nature. Lucetta's dress, the environment and the time of day where the sun is like 'a drop of blood on an eyelid' all help in constructing what is a particularly good example of Hardy's technique of *sympathetic background*.

toilette A woman's preparation of herself to face the world – her dress, hair, complexion etc.

Chapter 36

When Lucetta returns home she finds Jopp waiting outside her house with a request that she ask Farfrae to support his application to be employed as working partner to a corn-merchant. She refuses to have anything to do with it. Back in his lodgings,

Henchard asks Jopp to deliver the parcel of letters to Mrs Farfrae; on his way Jopp is met by some of the local characters and persuaded to spend some time in the 'Peter's Finger Inn'. Before long the parcel has been opened and the contents are public property, though the information in them is circumstantial only. The letters are considered to be an excellent foundation for a 'skimmity ride', and a passing visitor who hears of the plans contributes a sovereign towards the cost. Jopp re-seals the parcel and delivers it next morning; within an hour Lucetta has burned the contents.

Commentary

Jopp is perhaps the one character in *The Mayor of Casterbridge* whom it is hard to like. He is not really a villain – he is not developed enough by Hardy to achieve that distinction – and though he is unfairly treated by Henchard in Chapter 10 he never occupies more than the edge of the action. Less interesting than the other members of Hardy's rustic chorus, he is here a tool for carrying the story further forward. Lucetta's refusal to speak on his behalf to Farfrae is included, to give Jopp a motive for the enmity that results in the skimmity ride. A good deal of the chapter is spent in describing the milieu of Mixen Lane. Hardy clearly feels affection for this focus of the lower element of Casterbridge life, and it serves to give us some of his most slyly humorous writing – usually distinctly patronizing and relying perhaps on the fact that the real place and characters he described were already things of the past as he wrote about them. The introduction of the stranger is Hardy's attempt to make the return of Newson less of a shock; Jopp's role at the end as at the beginning is that of a somewhat anaemic villain.

iron dogs Bars that support the ends of the logs in a wood fire.
tyro Novice.
congeries Collection.
Adullam Resort of those in distress. (1 Samuel, 22, 1–2).
bibbing Tippling, drinking.
lifeholders The lease of their house and land lasted for life.
copyholders The holders held no original deeds confirming their tenure, only a copy of the manorial court-roll.
like Ashton . . . Ravenswood At the end of Scott's *The Bride of*

Lammermoor Colonel Ashton was waiting to fight a duel with Ravenswood. Ravenswood was riding across the sands towards him when he suddenly disappeared, swallowed by quicksands.

swingels The swinging parts of flails (hand-threshing tools).

blower A metal plate put over the upper part of a fireplace to draw up the fire.

oven-pyle A shovel for putting loaves into the oven.

skimmity-ride Sometimes called skimmington-ride; a custom whereby if a married person created a scandal, the transgressing parties were carried in effigy around the town. There is one moulded in plaster in Montacute House near Yeovil.

Chapter 37

A member of the royal family is passing through Casterbridge and an address of welcome is prepared. Henchard asks if he may join the welcoming party, but his request is refused because he is no longer a member of the council. He therefore prepares his own welcome, and at the crucial moment steps forward waving a homespun union jack, only to be pulled back and ordered away by Farfrae. Plans to hold the skimmity ride are well under way, and Solomon Longways resolves to write a note to those most likely to be affected, advising them to keep away.

Commentary

This episode marks the nadir of Henchard's standing in the town. In the clothes he had worn as mayor, now desperately shabby, he appears ludicrous and all the more pathetic because he seems not to realize it. By contrast Lucetta is trying hard – perhaps too hard – to behave in the way her new civic position requires, and is not above distorting the truth in the process. The shine of her reputation is beginning to be dimmed somewhat among the townspeople, through envy of her and of Farfrae, and neither she nor Nance Mockridge emerge from the episode particularly creditably. In contrast with this, Solomon Longways and Christopher Coney, by resolving to send warning 'to those most concerned' show a human and endearing side that is not given to Jopp.

an immense engineering work Hardy is probably referring to the construction of the breakwater at Portland Harbour. At that time th railway was about to reach Dorchester.

third King George ... Kings Arms George III liked to spend time at Weymouth and would no doubt have passed through Dorchester en route.

fête carillonée (Fr.) literally a holiday when the bells would be rung – hence a splendid public holiday.

cortège (Fr.) procession.

saw that his Calphurnia's cheek was pale As at the beginning of Shakespeare's *Julius Caesar*; Caesar is in a public place with a great crowd following and Brutus notices that the cheek of Calpurnia, Caesar's wife, is pale. (*Julius Caesar* I,2,185).

heavily as Pharaoh's chariots In pursuit of the Israelites (Exodus, 14,9).

go snacks wi'en i.e. share his table.

hontish Haughty.

toppered Brought low, tumbled down.

pat Fitting, apt.

Chapter 38

After his public humiliation Henchard goes to Farfrae's house with a request that Farfrae come out to see him; he then ties his own arm to his body and waits on the top floor. When Farfrae arrives he tells him that they are about to fight until one of them is thrown out of the open door forty feet to the ground. With his strength he is able to force Farfrae to the edge, but he is unable to bring himself to take his life, and flings himself into a corner. Farfrae goes down the ladder, and shortly afterwards leaves in a gig. Henchard hears the sounds of a band but thinks nothing of it.

Commentary

Henchard's actions are those of a desperately unhappy man, but one who has no notion of what he really wants or how to go about it if he had. His motives, as ever, are confused; there is vindictiveness in his desire to kill Farfrae, and compassion in the fact that he is fair-minded enough to tie his hand behind his back to make the coming fight more evenly balanced. The melting of his resolve in the face of Farfrae's song and his inability to kill him once he has him completely in his power are further points in Henchard's favour. Farfrae too deserves praise for his reaction; he seems ready to take each meeting with Henchard as a new one, and does not bear any grudge about Henchard's recent behaviour in front of royalty. He even seems concerned that Henchard has chosen to work on a day when the rest of his employees have a holiday.

Weltlust (Germ.) Love of worldly pleasure.

Chapter 39

Farfrae is about to set out for Budmouth when he receives a note asking him to go to Weatherbury. The note is a device to remove him from Casterbridge while the skimmington-ride takes place. Lucetta, hearing a commotion, is anxious to see what is causing it, and looks out only to see herself in effigy tied to an effigy of Henchard. She falls to the floor in a seizure; the doctor is called and pronounces that it is serious. He orders a servant to fetch Farfrae from Budmouth. One of the magistrates realizes what is going on and goes in search of the constables, intending to put a stop to the skimmington-ride, but he finds that the whole procession seems to have vanished.

Commentary

The skimmington-ride was an old west-country tradition and Hardy took evident delight in describing this one. It is here that his sense of humour emerges most forcibly in writing about the way in which the various instruments have been concealed – a continuation of the scene set in Chapter 36. The constables again are the targets of mild satire, as they appear totally ineffective. The contrast between Elizabeth-Jane and Lucetta is again instructive: the one is collected and decisive where the other is emotional and melodramatic. Lucetta pays a heavy price for her reluctance to tell her husband the whole of the background of her relationship with Henchard before their marriage. The reader guesses that her pregnancy has been one of the factors in making the impact of the skimmity ride so grave, but Hardy does not state this explicitly until the next chapter.

she really seemed to have no cause for fear Such statements as this are, in Hardy, nearly always ironic.
the malter's chimbley The chimney of the maltings (which was interrupting her view).
cleavers Choppers, axes.

crouds Fiddles.

humstrums Hurdy-gurdies.

serpents Old wind instruments, often used in church bands.

felo de se (Lat.) suicide, 'while of sound mind'.

soughed Sighed (as the wind went through them).

like the crew of 'Comus' From a masque of this name by John Milton (1608–74). Comus was a magician accompanied by a crew of noisy revellers who would disappear at his bidding.

Chapter 40

Henchard is very unsettled. He sees the skimmity-ride, goes home, and then quickly calls to see Elizabeth-Jane, only to be told that she has gone to Mrs Farfrae's. Following her there, he hears what has happened. He tells the servant that Farfrae has gone to Weatherbury rather than Budmouth, but no-one will believe him. He decides to go along the Weatherbury road to tell Farfrae himself, and meets him returning; but Farfrae too will not believe him and persists in his intention to go home via Mellstock. Henchard returns to tell the household that Farfrae cannot be home for another two hours, and when he goes to his lodging, he is told by Jopp that a sea-captain has been looking for him. Farfrae returns home in time to comfort his wife before she dies.

Commentary

All Henchard's good intentions are frustrated. The fault is of course ultimately his own, but the efforts he puts into making amends – in walking or running a considerable distance to warn Farfrae, and walking up and down outside Farfrae's house through the night – go a long way to remind the reader of the admirable side of his character. For the section on Lucetta's illness and death, Hardy uses a different technique. His usual stance is that of the writer who is omniscient – who knows every secret motive of his characters' actions. Here he drops this, at least apparently, while he suggests how much of her liaison with Henchard Lucetta revealed to her husband on her last night on earth. One notices too the economy with which the reader is informed of Lucetta's death – by the quiet removal of the cloth that had been muffling the door-knocker.

Over this repentant sinner . . . heaven A slightly altered version of
  Luke, 15, 7.
a less scrupulous Job See Job, 3, 1–16.
Lucifer The morning star.

Revision questions on Chapters 34–40

1 How does Hardy use Mixen Lane and its inhabitants?

2 Contrast the impulsively rash with the impulsively generous
aspects of Henchard in these chapters.

3 Compare Lucetta's visit to the Ring with Susan's in Chapter
11.

4 How does Hardy use the royal visit in terms of the ways it
affects Henchard and Farfrae and as a comment on small-town
politics?

5 Who is responsible for Lucetta's death?

6 'The skimmity-ride is an interesting description of an old folk
custom.' Is it any more than this?

Chapter 41

Elizabeth-Jane goes to visit Henchard and he persuades her to
rest. Tired from her exertions, she falls asleep while he is preparing breakfast. Meanwhile Newson pays Henchard a visit in
order to enquire after his wife and daughter; impulsively Henchard tells him that she is dead, and he leaves sorrowfully.
Frightened that what he has just done will be discovered, and
seeing no future for himself, Henchard thinks of committing
suicide by drowning himself in a deep pool in the river. He is
prevented from doing so when he sees what he thinks is himself
floating in the water – in reality the effigy of himself that had
been used in the skimmity-ride. He returns home to be recon-
ciled to Elizabeth-Jane, who offers to go and care for him; her
offer restores some of his self-respect.

Commentary

The reconciliation of Elizabeth-Jane and Henchard promises to
be one of the most moving in the book, but there are already

hints that it will not last long because of the return of Newson. That Elizabeth-Jane should be actually in the next room when he is told that his daughter is dead is a touch typical of Hardy (there is a similar incident in *The Return of the Native*), while Henchard's immediate and instinctive wish to cling on to the only thing that gives him some hope in life is understandable even if it cannot win our approval. Indeed his behaviour here is directly comparable with that of Lucetta earlier who is also ready to forget moral imperatives in the interests of her own selfish wishes. The chapter ends with one of Hardy's most macabre scenes – the discovery of the effigy of himself floating in the water that makes Henchard think he has seen an agency of doom. Again one thinks of Lucetta's emotional reaction to the sight of her own effigy and of how for her too Elizabeth-Jane has been the voice of common sense. The suggestion is that Henchard and Lucetta were better matched than perhaps either had realized.

to the east of Casterbridge . . . a very fugue of sounds A paragraph where Hardy combines his love of music with his love of Dorset to telling effect.

Chapter 42

A considerable time elapses and Henchard is set up by the Council as a seed merchant; Elizabeth-Jane takes care of him, and it might appear that his tribulations are over. He is nevertheless disturbed by the interest that Farfrae seems to be taking in her and fears that he may lose her; he thinks about telling Farfrae that she is not after all his child, but banishes the thought in disgust at his own selfishness.

Commentary

On an initial reading of *The Mayor of Casterbridge* one's first impression is that the narrative moves relentlessly and at a fairly constant pace. This chapter indicates that this is by no means always the case, for almost a year elapses before the next significant development in the story. Henchard's establishment as the proprietor of a small seed shop suggests that his trials and tribulations are over, and part of the reason for this is that he no longer seems the tempestuous character that he was in the middle of the novel. Again there are hints that more is yet to come: Newson, after all, despite his apparently conclusive departure, is still alive and travelling, and the regards which Farfrae is starting to pay towards Elizabeth-Jane are a further reminder of his tactlessness as well as a reminder that fate seems destined to throw the two men against one another in so many different ways during the course of the story. The ending of the chapter too is a reminder that the driving force behind the book is tragedy.

'in his own grey style' A quotation from Shelley's *Epipsychidion* (line 55).

Juno's bird The peacock.

Argus eyes Argus had a hundred eyes and was set to watch the nymph Io by Juno. Mercury succeeded in sending him to sleep and slew him, after which his eyes were put on the tail of Juno's sacred peacock.

solicitus timor (Lat.) Anxious fear: a phrase from Ovid's *Epistolae Heroidum*.

locus standi (Lat.) Recognized position.

Chapter 43

The attachment between Farfrae and Elizabeth-Jane develops, and Henchard is led to contemplate what he will do when they are married. He decides that he can bear the humiliation; but one day while on the ramparts of a nearby hill-fort he sees with his telescope that Newson is returning to Casterbridge. He decides to leave the town before Elizabeth-Jane discovers the truth; he walks away dressed much the same as when he arrived twenty-five years before. Farfrae meets Elizabeth-Jane as she returns from bidding Henchard farewell, and takes her to his house; she finds her real father – Newson – sitting there. Only now does she realize that he is her father, and finds it impossible to forgive Henchard's deceit. Preparations are made for the wedding.

Commentary

The chapter starts with more gentle satire at the expense of the Casterbridge beauties each of whom considered herself to be the only one that Fate had marked out as a consort for Farfrae.

Perspective is restored in the wisdom of Christopher Coney, who was earlier something of a buffoon, but who here can see the situation more clearly than anyone else. Henchard's reaction to the catastrophe of Newson's reappearance is most moving. He immediately forsakes the haven that he had enjoyed for the previous year, and the description of his departure from Casterbridge is all the more powerful because it echoes the description at the start of the novel as well as the account of his arrival at Casterbridge. Hardy leaves it to the reader to make the points of comparison, and as a result of this understatement the episode gains greatly in its effect. Two contrasts are especially important; the first is one of character where Newson, who has been directly involved with Henchard only twice, is ready to call him 'poor Henchard' and reluctantly acknowledges his own part in his opposite number's misfortunes (in stark contrast to Farfrae). The second is one of structure as the preparations for the wedding and the joy of Elizabeth-Jane's meeting with her father are set against the lonely departure of Henchard from the town.

pillow A malapropism for 'pillar'.
éclat (Fr.) Distinction.
Mai Dun A large hillfort dating from before the arrival of the Romans and about a mile from Dorchester; known today as 'Maiden Castle'.
Via (Lat.) the High Road.
knee-knaps Leather pads worn over the knees.
Cain See Genesis, 4, 8–15.
schiedam A drink named from the town in Holland where it used chiefly to be made.

Chapter 44

Henchard goes fifty miles and eventually arrives at Weydon-Priors, where he relives the events described in the novel's opening chapters. His thoughts keep turning to Elizabeth-Jane and, working as a hay-trusser, he traces the edge of a circular route which has Casterbridge as its centre. He hears from a waggoner's wife of Elizabeth-Jane's impending marriage and decides to go back. He arrives at the house as the celebrations are in progress, with a caged bird as a present for Elizabeth-Jane. She rejects him, and he vows never to trouble her more.

Commentary

Henchard feels he is impelled into a predestined circle of events. This was hinted at in the end of the previous chapter, when he leaves Casterbridge, but his revisiting of the fairground at Weydon-Priors further emphasizes this. His complete hopelessness, however, indicates that his path now can only lead downwards. Hardy explicitly states what has been implicit for a good deal of the novel: 'the ingenious machinery contrived by the gods for reducing human possibilities of amelioration to a minimum stood in the way of all that'. The symbol of the caged finch stands powerfully for the character of the man who bought it, and the extensive descriptions of the merrymaking at the wedding are inserted the more to emphasize his isolation and misery. Even here it is characteristic of Henchard not to make any excuses on his own behalf, and to be his own severest critic.

ballet-sheet Ballad-sheet. See Chapter 1.
pixy-ring A ring of dark-coloured grass, common on old pasture and heaths.
centripetal Tending towards the centre (the opposite of centrifugal).
pari passu (Lat.) at the same pace.
without horses i.e. by rail.
mid Might.
waggon-tilt Coverings on the waggon.
Martin's day 11 November.
the drag An iron shoe fitted under a wheel when descending a steep hill to make it drag rather than revolve.
a Samson shorn A strong man deprived of his strength. See Judges, 16, 15–21.
emolliated (A word seldom used nowadays) softened.
out-Farfraed Farfrae in saltatory intenseness. A quotation modified from *Hamlet* (III, 2, 17), which means that the enthusiasm with which he danced surpassed Farfrae's.
'the shade . . . upthrown' A quotation from Shelley's *The Revolt of Islam* (1. 3245); the darkness of his own personality had made him want to take Newson's daughter.

Chapter 45

A week after her wedding Elizabeth-Jane finds the cage Henchard had brought with a dead goldfinch inside. For a further three weeks she does not find out why it is there until a maid tells her that Henchard had left it; and her heart softens towards him. She and Farfrae go to look for him, and at the end of a long search find him in a dilapidated cottage, cared for by Abel Whittle – but he has been dead for half an hour. Whittle has followed him because he had been generous to his mother when she was alive. They read Henchard's will, pencilled on a scrap of paper and pinned to the head of the bed. Elizabeth-Jane is greatly moved by his death, and though she settles into the life of a prosperous merchant's wife, she is aware that good-fortune is exceedingly fickle.

Commentary

The power of the novel's ending does not come from the search for Henchard – that is fairly perfunctorily treated – but from the setting of his death and from Whittle's long description of how it had come about. In this Hardy shows great skill; in the hand of the omniscient novelist, particularly one with Hardy's tendency to display the width of his knowledge, it might have seemed an anticlimax but, in the hands of an illiterate countryman who emphasizes Henchard's virtues, it gains greatly in sincerity. Henchard's death seems tragic when measured against a Farfrae who can talk about the search as 'making a hole in a sovereign' and greet Whittle's information that a man was about to come to measure Henchard's body with 'Dear me – is that so!' The last paragraphs show Hardy writing in a vein that is constricted and distinctly ill-at-ease, which contrasts greatly with the simplicity of Whittle's speech and Henchard's will; and though they ostensibly apply to Elizabeth-Jane, there has been enough evidence elsewhere to make the reader think that they reflect Hardy's own attitude towards existence.

antipodean absences Absences in penal settlements in Australia.
half-yearly occurrences The assizes were held twice a year.
Minerva-eyes Wise, thoughtful eyes; Minerva was goddess of wisdom.
Diana Multimammia Diana of the many breasts – a goddess of human fertility.
supinely Lying on the back. Here the meaning is: pointing upwards.
fond Silly.
traps Pieces of rickety furniture.
Capharnaum Where Jesus went to live: the 'region and shadow of death' as prophesied in Isaiah 9, 2. See Matthew, 4, 13–16.
discovering In its old meaning of disclosing.

Revision questions on Chapters 41–45

1 Compare Henchard's state of mind when he considers drowning himself, with his state of mind in the last chapter.

2 How does the serenity of Henchard's seed shop seem constantly under threat?

3 Does Hardy make any attempt to present Newson as a convincing character?

4 What use does Hardy make of contrast in Chapter 44?

5 What is achieved by putting the account of Henchard's last weeks into the mouth of Abel Whittle?

6 Does Elizabeth-Jane seem less sympathetic in the last two chapters?

Hardy's art in *The Mayor of Casterbridge*
The characters

Michael Henchard

He . . . stood like a dark ruin, obscured by 'the shade from his own soul upthrown'

There is only one real character in *The Mayor of Casterbridge*; though in the course of the novel there are at least two mayors, no reader can seriously suppose that the novel is about Donald Farfrae. We are never told exactly when Henchard's term as mayor ends; it seems to subside when Farfrae's star rises about half-way through the book. Once we look at the overall structure of the story we can see that Henchard's moment of supreme power is relatively brief; that Hardy barely gives himself time to establish his 'man of character' as the chief magistrate of the town before he starts to undermine his position and quietly to remind us of the flaws that are eventually to destroy him.

The picture of Henchard as it is first set down in Chapter 1 is a telling one. His appearance is impressive and there is pride in the way he dresses and walks – he is after all a 'skilled countryman' rather than a general labourer, but he is also totally self-contained, reading a ballad-sheet and not communicating with his wife at all. For a man of twenty-one this is surprising, and it is to prove characteristic. His black moods seem like an extension of his swarthy countenance, and if it is a truism to say that everyone has two sides to his personality, Henchard's two sides seem polarized more than those of most people. Most tragic of all for him is that there seems to be no middle ground between the two, and his sense of humour is almost non-existent. There are many incidents in the story which, if treated slightly differently, could have been very amusing – one thinks of the Whittle episode, the cat and mouse game that Lucetta plays with him and he with her, the furmity woman's appearance in court – but when Henchard laughs, his laugh is aggressive and indicative of deep insecurity. Thus his drinking, both at the start of the novel and twenty-one years later, is immoderate; it is the action of a man wishing to drown his sorrows and to be revenged on a world that treats him as it does. Susan's act – in steering him away from the tent selling beer and cider and into that selling furmity – results in the disastrous sale. This is in the best Aristotelian tradition and a piece of typical Hardy irony.

The next morning Henchard is filled with the confusion of the previous day's imperfectly remembered events, but he is collected enough to blame Susan's naiveté for what had happened – though this disguises a deep sense of shame that shows he is aware the fault was his own; his oath (to cease drinking for twenty-one years) is an outward expression of this. Hardy tells us that 'there was something fetichistic in this man's beliefs' and we can see that for the first half of the novel he rules his life, subsequent to the opening chapter, by a rigid, indeed puritanical morality that forms a framework for his conduct. His personality is ruled by emotion rather than reason, and for him and for countless thousands of people whose intellect is not powerful but whose industry and ambition are great, he succeeds in framing a code of morality that brings him success if not affection. The fetichistic quality emerges in a number of ways – his oath is to abstain from alcohol for as long as he had already been alive; the sending of five guineas to Susan on her reappearance; waiting for exactly twenty-one years then suddenly cutting the stays that had kept his life in compass. He does not enjoy it; at the mayoral banquet his glass of water is on the table in despite of what he wants, and as he later says to Farfrae 'and though I am sometimes that dry in the dog days that I could drink a quarter-barrel to the pitching, I think o' my oath and touch no strong drink at all.' It certainly earns him the slightly fearful respect of the townspeople.

Henchard's appearance at the dinner in the 'King's Arms' is the zenith of his fortunes, and he does not stay in this position for long before events and personalities start to gnaw at the foundations of his prosperity. To an alert reader his nervousness when he is attacked over the grown wheat shows him looking everywhere for such attacks and reacting to them with brittle aggressiveness. A chapter later he has started the swing to the opposite pole that is to result within two chapters more in his offering Farfrae lodging in his own house, offering him two breakfasts and not long afterwards telling him some of his most intimate secrets. This generosity of spirit is endearing if rash; when he meets Susan to confess his sins in humility and wishes to expiate the action of Chapter 1, he has gone a long way towards gaining the reader's sympathy. When we further hear of the black moods 'where the world seems to have the blackness of hell, and, like Job, I could curse the day that gave me birth' that sympathy is increased, and Farfrae with his 'Ah no I never feel like that' seems pale beside him.

But in employing Farfrae Henchard has totally disregarded his commitment to Jopp. In following his impulse he has not been very fair, and there are plenty of hints that this has happened frequently; we are told that many of the townspeople had been made to smart under his tongue, his treatment of Whittle is as Farfrae says, tyrannical, and when Farfrae parts from him and sets up his own business, the speed with which Henchard's customers come over to him is yet further indication. His lack of sensitivity to the feelings of others is evidence of selfishness natural enough in a deeply introverted man but selfishness nevertheless; for instance, one of his main concerns upon having Susan restored to him is that no one in the town should know about their past.

At the best of times Henchard leads a lonely life, in the home and outside it. In the first chapter he is walking along a road out of fellowship with his wife; after the return of his wife and stepdaughter he provides well for them (ornately and lavishly it seems to Susan) but gives them no companionship. His contacts with Elizabeth-Jane are occasional and formal, and up to the time when she leaves home he is quite unaware of her interests – he has no idea of how hard she has tried to fit herself to her new position. When he sees it, it is too late; he has failed to give her affection and interest and once her mother is dead there is nobody else at all who can help her until Lucetta arrives. He is unable to discern why Lucetta behaves as she does, or to understand why Elizabeth-Jane behaves as she does when she is in love with Farfrae. In telling Farfrae the secrets of his past life and his present dilemma over two innocent women he admits 'I feel it a great relief, Farfrae, to tell some friend o' this!' When he is annoyed with Farfrae some time later, his anger imputes wrong motives to Farfrae's actions, and he charges him (or affects to charge him) with taking advantage of him because he knows his secrets.

Henchard asks for Farfrae's advice, but only in the hope of support to prove himself right, not because he really wants it. When it does not agree with what he intends to do he as quickly rejects it: 'Never! I am not going to let her know the truth.'

Having appointed Farfrae as his manager Henchard is incap able of leaving everything to him. He wants to interfere and he is only too conscious of his standing with the employees; when Farfrae overrides him in instructing Abel Whittle to go home and get his trousers, Hardy tells us that 'the seed that was to lift the foundation of this friendship was at that moment taking root in a chink of its structure'. Yet in fact it had taken root much earlier, when Henchard appointed him, as he did not have the foresight to see that a man who gave him advice on how to restore 'growed wheat' would be likely to be better informed on numerous other matters and would in fact surpass him. The 'northern insight matched against southron doggedness' could have only one outcome, and when it does, Henchard behaves like a spoilt child: over the Whittle affair, in organizing a rival (and as he thought, superior) festivity to Farfrae's, in dismissing Farfrae, in forbidding him to see Elizabeth-Jane, in the mis- guided attempt to drive Farfrae out of business, and most pointedly, in his comments on the new seed-drill. His generosity in trying to make amends to Lucetta for his behaviour towards her and his attempt to return her letters to the Antelope Hotel are admirable; his pique in refusing to see her when he has had a slight rebuff is to contribute towards his undoing.

From this point onwards Henchard's decline is rapid. The melodramatic visit to Fall, which propels him into the disastrous commercial dealings leading to his bankruptcy, introduces a sudden quickening in the pace of the story. In this section too we are reminded of the two sides of Henchard's character – he wins us over by his honesty when facing his creditors; by denying nothing of the furmity woman's allegations; by his brave hand- ling of the savage bull. He repels us by his vindictive intention towards Lucetta over her papers; by the constant threat of physical violence he poses towards Farfrae (which at first only Elizabeth-Jane can see, but which very nearly results in the death of Farfrae during their struggle in the hay-loft).

The key chapter in determining our attitude towards Hen- chard at this stage of the novel is that which shows him taking strong drink once more. His impulse is totally self-destructive as he asks the church choir to perform Psalm 109. He maintains, as Farfrae and Lucetta pass by, that the words are directed at Farfrae but there is more than a suggestion that they are directed at himself. He joins with alacrity the select society that gazes into the river at Grey's Bridge; his bitter sarcasm towards Lucetta as she passes him in the yard behind what had been his own house is delivered with a perverse masochistic enjoyment. We see in fact the steady return of the Henchard who had sold his wife at Weydon-Priors, in that his behaviour is cruel or threatening towards Farfrae, Elizabeth-Jane, Lucetta, Newson and Whittle. While Newson has the magnanimity to describe as 'a joke' the manner in which he was tricked by Henchard into thinking Elizabeth-Jane was dead, the reader and Elizabeth-Jane, when she eventually finds out, know him too well ever to think that it was intended as a joke.

In Chapters 41 and 42 we see a Henchard who apparently has for the first time found real happiness; he has Elizabeth-Jane to care for him; he has regained a modicum of stability in the small shop with which he has been provided; and we gather that almost a year passes in this relatively untroubled state. Yet even the serenity of this period is under constant threat − that Elizabeth-Jane will discover the lie he has told to Newson, and that the feeling Elizabeth-Jane displays for Farfrae will remove her from him again. We note the selfish fear that this engenders and which prompts Henchard to consider telling Farfrae that she is legally nobody's child. That he curses himself for thoughts like this and does not put them into practice is to his credit.

The sudden and improbable return of Newson puts an end to this brief period of prosperity, and Henchard's exit from Caster-bridge is that of a man whose mind is rigid in its mould; indeed his return to Weydon-Priors is an attempt to provide some sort of a framework for his life. Hardy emphasizes the pathos of his departure partly by making the details of his clothing corres-pond so closely to those he wore at the opening of the book, and in the mementoes of Elizabeth-Jane that he carries with him.

His determination to go to her wedding-festivities is an act that is typically impulsive; and it produces the only time in the novel where the reader feels more for Henchard than for Elizabeth-Jane. The present of the caged bird takes Hardy dan-gerously close to sentimentality, but he ultimately avoids it by using it in a way that is decidedly practical, in letting Elizabeth-Jane deduce what had happened on the night of her wedding four weeks before.

The words 'I'll never trouble 'ee again, Elizabeth-Jane − no, not to my dying day! Good night. Good-bye!' mark the last appearance of Henchard in the novel, and the action of the last chapter is mainly concerned with Elizabeth-Jane's and Farfrae's search for him, together with their chance discovery of Whittle and the hovel that Henchard had died in shortly before. It comes as something of a surprise to realize that Henchard at his death is only a little over forty-four years old; and if his death is a convenient way of ending the book there is nothing but despair in the way it is brought about. His will is a grotesque parody of the way the psalms are written – an indication that he has lost the will to live, and that even the thought of suicide by drowning that had crossed his mind four chapters before is now superfluous and unnecessary.

Farfrae

That will make a hole in a sovereign

Farfrae is introduced in Chapter 6 as one of those who was a witness of the mayoral banquet, and he continues to be prominent for the rest of the novel. He is in every way a contrast to Henchard – 'ruddy and of a fair countenance, bright-eyed and slight in build', and the contrast is maintained to such a degree that it sometimes seems almost contrived. His situation after all is exactly parallel to that of Henchard twenty years before – an impecunious young man who is seeking his fortune in a strange town. He has an air of romance about him as he comes from parts far distant at a time when to travel was comparatively rare, and his freshness is well conveyed by the songs he sings about the country which he is in fact quite happy to be leaving. His first act in the story is a generous one; he offers to help Henchard out of his embarrassment over the grown wheat, and explains the process to him in full without any hope of reward or of apparent interest in the matter. His modesty is reflected in the fact that he is in no way showy, carries his possessions in a carpet bag and chooses to stay at an inn that is less than the best Casterbridge can offer. It is soon plain that his decisions are made coolly and that he is prepared to manage Henchard's business to the best of his ability and with 'genial modesty' – qualities that are well displayed when he meets Elizabeth-Jane in the barn following Susan's message to both of them.

Henchard's business prospers under Farfrae's management

and it is soon clear that he is well liked in the town; the snatches of conversation during the entertainment he had arranged for the national holiday are proof of that, as is the fact that the townspeople quickly turn to him rather than to Henchard when they want any advice. It is jealousy over this as much as the growing spirit of independence exemplified by his countermanding Henchard's orders to Whittle that makes Henchard dismiss him. When he sets up his own business he behaves honourably in at first refusing to take away any of Henchard's customers. His conversation with Lucetta where he describes his business successes (Chp. 23) reveals a boyish enthusiasm as much as the successes reveal the shrewd businessman. Up to this point the reader can share the townspeople's enthusiasm for him.

In affairs of the heart he is at first more calculating. He is ready to neglect the worthier but less immediately attractive Elizabeth-Jane for the wealthy but relatively shallow Lucetta, and in doing so he begins to behave in a way that is apparently calculated to emphasize the reversal of his and Henchard's relative positions. Not content with superseding him as the main corn factor of the town, Farfrae woos and later marries Henchard's intended wife. He buys and goes to live in Henchard's house; he buys his furniture and only later does Henchard find out that it was with the intention of giving it back to him. After Lucetta's death Farfrae marries the only person Henchard loves unreservedly, Elizabeth-Jane. This serves to confirm that Farfrae is a man whose level of feeling is shallow compared with that of Henchard. If Henchard sometimes feels that he 'could curse the day that gave me birth', Farfrae's reply: 'Ah, no, I never feel like that,' and Hardy's comment on him in the last chapter: 'Although Farfrae had never so passionately liked Henchard as Henchard had liked him, he had, on the other hand, never so passionately hated in the same direction as his former friend had done', all indicate that he is lacking in Henchard's warmth; he seems positively emotionally anaemic beside him.

As his wealth and position increase, the reader finds it harder to respond to him with quite the enthusiasm that he attracted earlier. Yet in many ways this is irrational, as one can find many acts of kindness or forbearance in him: the purchase of the carter with his old father so that the lovers shall not be separated; the move that comes from him to set up Henchard in a small seed business; the purchase of Henchard's furniture;

offering him employment in his own firm; and his moderate reaction to the interruption of the royal welcome. After the fight in the loft Farfrae could very well have taken legal action against Henchard but he does not do so. The reason for all this is clearly that he is being used as a contrast with Henchard, and his character is not allowed to develop if it appears to threaten this role.

Lastly, there is his role as a Scot. Many from north of the border criticized the character soon after the book was published, as bearing little relation to a real Scot, either in accent or behaviour. Hardy's answer was that Farfrae was a Scotsman as seen by a southerner. Although he went to some pains to check that the dialect was reasonably authentic it is perhaps relevant to point out that the prototype for Farfrae was probably a Yorkshireman.

Susan Henchard

As guiltless o' wrong-doing as a saint in the clouds

Susan has the strangest experiences of any character in the book, in that she is married twice to the same man with nineteen years intervening. Her appearance at the opening is almost that of a beast of burden as she says nothing and has nothing said to her until she guides her husband into the furmity tent in an attempt to keep him away from strong drink. She is understandably concerned about where they are going for their night's lodging before events overtake her and Newson lays his money on the table. The spirit she shows in her angry speech and the way she throws her wedding ring at her husband are clear indications that the cowed personality she displays at the start is not the whole Susan.

This impression is confirmed when we see her nineteen years later. She has had the energy to search for her husband after having lived in a variety of places, lost one child and had another. As the story continues it appears that she is single-minded in attempting to secure the future of her child, as she arranges the assignation with Farfrae, hoping that it will be the start of a romance. She studiously keeps from Henchard the real details of the girl he supposes to be his daughter; even Newson believes that she could write her own name and no more, yet she had penned quite a considerable letter to Henchard while on her deathbed. She has also concealed from Elizabeth-Jane the true facts behind her birth and upbringing, merely showing unease when Henchard requests that the girl's name be altered from Newson to Henchard. Susan appears for less than a third of the novel, and this is not enough space for Hardy to be able fully to develop her character.

Lucetta

I'll love where I choose!

The start of Lucetta's history is never made clear; we are told that her name was Le Sueur, that she came from Jersey, that Michael Henchard had met her there and that a romance had blossomed between them when she had nursed him during an illness. Her first arrival in Casterbridge never takes place as planned because of the legacy she has received from the Bristol aunt; and when she does arrive it is with the firm intention of cutting herself off from her past now that she has become wealthy. Her discovery of Elizabeth-Jane and the friendship she shows towards her are, it soon transpires, means to establish contact with Henchard, and when it appears that Elizabeth-Jane and Henchard are estranged she promptly breaks down in tears.

We are never told the exact nature of the indiscretions between her and Henchard, but her indiscreet letters and her behaviour towards Farfrae once she has met him are the actions of a coquette — 'to Elizabeth-Jane it was as plain as the town pump that Donald and Lucetta were incipient lovers' — as is symbolized by her intense love of fashionable clothes, and by the intense nervousness she shows (Ch. 24) as to whether her charms are starting to fade. She rebuffs Henchard's first approach in order to increase his ardour, and by the time she is ready to receive him she has transferred her affections to Farfrae. In receiving him we note the studied actress who arranges herself in an impressive pose on a settee. When later she goes to beg Henchard to return her letters, her attire is chosen with a sense of theatre. Broken promises mean little to her; she possesses none of the firm integrity of Elizabeth-Jane. Her wedding to Farfrae has a hint of deceit about it; she is unwilling to be married openly, but quietly arranges that the ceremony be performed at Port-Bredy, fifteen miles away.

Once Lucetta is married her past starts to catch up with her.

She is less than totally frank with her husband, mainly because she is terrified that she may lose him; she pays dearly for this as she listens on the stairs in fear that Henchard may reveal her secret. Her avowal of her feelings in letters seems strangely rash and is to result in her undoing when Jopp is responsible for the public revelation of their contents in the 'Peter's Finger Inn'. The jealousy she incurs from the townspeople emerges forcibly during the episode of the royal visit, and it is plain that the gloss bestowed on her by a fashionable match has worn off fairly rapidly. Her collapse and death when she is aware that her effigy is one of the objects carried in the skimmity-ride suggests that she cannot live without an image.

Elizabeth-Jane

A girl characterized by earnestness and soberness of mien

Elizabeth-Jane is one of the most subtle characters in the novel. She is presented first in Chapter 3 almost as a little girl, following her mother in her search for Henchard; she is a little naive in her questions and full of curiosity to find out more about the strange relation whom they have come so far to see. She is shown early to be practical and humble since she is willing to take a menial position in order to make things easier for her mother.

As the story continues it becomes increasingly clear that she is used by Hardy to put over his point of view. Her morning walk takes her past many of the hidden gardens of Casterbridge on a bright day in autumn, and the brilliance of the flowers transfers itself to her. She comes into a world where for the first time in her life she can have money spent on her and Susan and she can forget about material wants, yet she remains moderate in her requests, and as her face fills outs and her physical attractions increase she is ready to heighten them in only very simple ways. There is considerable evidence that Hardy modelled her on one of his sisters, and it soon becomes clear that she is an admirable advertisement for the virtues of a morality that she puts over with conviction – and which would no doubt have earned the approval of the majority of the book's original readers.

Humility indeed is the keystone of Elizabeth-Jane's personality. She feels that she is uneducated and goes to great lengths to improve her mind by reading extensively. Her resigned acceptance of the faults that Henchard indicates makes her resolve to try all the harder to avoid using dialect words in her conversation. After her mother's death her resigned acceptance of his criticisms remind one of Desdemona in *Othello* – which Hardy saw while he was writing the book. Her removal to Lucetta's house is appealing to her as it will eliminate an evident irritation from Henchard and give her what promises to be a cheerful and cultural companion.

At High-Place Hall she becomes a foil to the flighty Lucetta, and if she cannot understand the complex relationship of Lucetta and Henchard she very early notices the signs that Lucetta is falling in love with Farfrae. She sees before anyone else that her stepfather's character is such that 'Farfrae's days as manager are numbered.' When she learns of Henchard's affair with Lucetta her judgment is forthright and immediate; 'You must remain a single woman'. The knowledge that Lucetta has married Farfrae makes her decide immediately that she can live at High-Place Hall no longer. It is significant that, meek and mild when anyone treats her roughly or inconsiderately, she is anything but meek and mild when anyone has done something she considers improper: 'any suspicion of impropriety was to Elizabeth-Jane like a red rag to a bull'.

Henchard's sudden decline into bankruptcy arouses her compassion, and she is insistent enough to go and see him when he wants to see nobody. Her relationship with him is a fairly close one, and by the time they settle down in the seed-shop, a very close one indeed. She is ready to forget his ill-treatment of her until the return of Newson; after her stepfather's sudden departure it is the discovery that he has lied over the return of her father that brings out the uncompromising streak we have already noted.

Her treatment of Henchard when he returns to her wedding festivities indicates a failure to understand why he has told this lie, and it is a failure that is to cause her much distress a month later when in silence she reads his will. It means that what might have been a happy ending to the novel as far as she is concerned remains muted.

Minor characters

Two named characters merit treatment in their own right – *Abel Whittle* and *Richard Newson*. Of these, *Abel Whittle* is perhaps the more important because he is individualized and given key roles at two points during the narrative. He first appears as one of Henchard's workmen with a chronic problem of getting up in the morning. Henchard's treatment of him is called tyrannical by Farfrae, but Whittle seems to accept it as his just desert. Its structural use in the novel is to provide the starting point for Henchard's and Farfrae's quarrel. His most important function, however, is to accompany Henchard as he leaves Casterbridge for the last time, to care for him for his last month on earth, and to report all this to Elizabeth-Jane and Farfrae. In Whittle's account Hardy showed a sure instinct; he was always at his best when rendering the conversation of ordinary people. Through Whittle's monologue Hardy prevents the book's end from being sentimental, as well as reminding us of Henchard's good points in his generosity towards Whittle's mother while she was alive.

Newson appears as a *deus ex machina* at the wife-sale and then disappears with his purchase for upwards of twenty years. We hear of him only at second hand, through Susan or Elizabeth-Jane, as a caring husband and father who, in the nature of his occupation, was often away from home. His rumoured drowning makes his return to life as surprising for his daughter as for the reader; and Hardy restores him anonymously and perfunctorily before he returns explicitly to look for his wife and daughter. He shows some naiveté in failing to investigate Susan's death and Elizabeth-Jane's supposed death, but is ready when he conveniently returns in Chapter 43 to regard the episode as a joke, something of a testimony to his good nature. He contributes his personality to the wedding festivities, then disappears to Budmouth after being unhappy over the loss of contact with the sea necessarily entailed in living ten miles away from it. He becomes something of a humorous caricature of a retired naval man, a contrast to his spectral entrance.

The chorus of townspeople which Hardy uses to comment on the action (though only rarely to take part in it) is one of his most interesting creations. They have been compared to the chorus of a Greek play, which performs an identical function, and as Hardy was influenced by Greek tragedy in his conception of the plot he may have had this in mind, though one remembers Shakespearian characters who are similarly used. Hardy's chorus shows invariable common sense; rough, earthy and often with unconscious humour, it serves to balance the novel in that without the chorus its sombre side might well be thought excessive. One remembers the comments outside the 'King's Arms' where Solomon Longways and Christopher Coney talk with deep respect about Henchard's vow just after Hardy as narrator has compared the dining councillors to nuzzling pigs. Also memorable are the lively comments on Farfrae in the 'Three Mariners' in Chapter 9; the observations on the newly celebrated marriage of Susan and Michael Henchard in Chapter 13; Christopher Coney's somewhat disrespectful use of the ounce pennies in Chapter 18; and the Mixen Lane section that leads into the skimmity-ride in Chapters 36 and 39.

Style

One is aware of a large number of different registers in the way Hardy's novels are written, and in the *Mayor of Casterbridge* he is constantly changing his point of view, his vocabulary and his technique. What binds them all together is his skill as a storyteller. He is able to produce a tale with a compelling quality; it is well adapted to a market that required a novel to be broken up into sections of roughly equal length, with variety in each one and with each chapter ending on a note that made the reader eager for the sequel.

The opening lines of the book show us the omniscient novelist looking on his characters as an invisible outsider, setting the atmosphere by his description of the dusty road and shabby clothes of the three people walking along. His eye roams over them, noting details of their behaviour towards each other, before it returns to tired nature in the last throes of summer with an aged bird to serenade the travellers.

Here the register suddenly changes and dialogue is introduced. This is one of Hardy's most characteristic features, as he had a taste for the dramatic that has always made his novels among the easier ones to dramatize. Plays of some of his novels were produced with his approval while he was still alive. Many of the novel's memorable moments are similarly presented, and here one may note immediately his unerring ear for dialect rendered unselfconsciously. Many others of his contemporaries would have been unable to do this without appearing patronizing, but Hardy is only rarely patronizing — one can recall his comments on the main instigators of the skimmity-ride as they put away their instruments before the arrival of the magistrates and constables.

The sudden introduction of the dialogue, which continues intermittently until the end of the chapter, makes one aware that when Hardy the narrator reappears his tone is that of an educated man using a wide and varied vocabularly. The contrast between 'no, not so much as a thatched hurdle' and "Twas no business of mine' with 'proceeded on their way' and 'exhibited and sold in the forenoon' shows the difference between a register dominated by words of Anglo-Saxon and those of Latinate origin.

This is a pointer to a feature of Hardy's personality, always retiring, intensely private, yet living by his pen, which necessitated a good deal of his most intimate thoughts becoming public. As soon as he became well known there began that intense public curiosity that all his life, he was anxious to frustrate. Hardy was educated first by his mother, then in a small school in Dorchester; to a large extent he was self-educated. He was always conscious of the educational opportunities obtained by his friend Horace Moule, son of the Rector of 'Durnover' or Fordington, and eager to show that he lacked nothing in learning by comparison. This appears very clearly in the *Mayor of Casterbridge*, as he is always comparing the events he describes to others with a literary or historical pedigree – every chapter needs footnotes that will explain these to a reader less widely read than he was. They are none the less examples of a hidden insecurity and perhaps under other circumstances might have been omitted.

Setting the novel in the fictionalized version of Dorchester gave him a marvellous opportunity. He was not the first to have used the area of his birth and upbringing as the centre of a novel – one thinks of Dickens, Emily Brontë, George Eliot and Mrs Gaskell – but he wrote of Dorset with an intensity that was new. One of his achievements is to have preserved the Dorchester of the mid-nineteenth century – the town he remembered from his boyhood – as a living entity, not as a museum-piece. To catalogue the various aspects of the town and its surroundings is superfluous, but the reader will notice close descriptions of buildings, many still standing though many are no more; of the close influence of the countryside as it appears on market day; in the items sold in the shops; the way the town's prosperity is heavily influenced by the effect of the weather on the agricultural community around it. Casterbridge's administration, law enforcement, merrymaking, churchgoing, business and history are all registered and integrated into the story so well that the cumulative picture is built up without the reader's being more than incidentally aware of it.

The breadth of Hardy's interests has already been noted in his close knowledge of architecture; but this is also true of painting and music, while the density of his knowledge of the Bible appears so evident that one can see that the agnostic Hardy, writing soon after that word was invented, knew the scriptures far better than the great majority of professed Christians. One notes the close indication of people's clothes at a time when, more than now, they pointed to a person's place in society: for example in the Candlemas hiring fair; in all the descriptions of Lucetta; and in the symbolism they present of Henchard's decline – his clothes may be genteel but their shabbiness and inappropriateness are deeply humiliating.

Yet the novel is emphatically not a museum-piece. It exists in its characters and particularly in that of Michael Henchard, who in his stature totally dominates the book. He is the focus of all the events that occur; his character is conveyed to the reader partly through his own words, partly through other characters' comments on him, and partly through the novelist's narrative, where comments on Henchard are regularly made. He is first described in the second paragraph of the book, a common practice in Victorian novels; but any extended description would slow up the action and after any character's significant traits have been mentioned the reader is left to fill in the details from his imagination. Similarly with Farfrae; Elizabeth-Jane (and therefore the reader) forms a general impression of him when she first sees him in the street (Ch.6) and the impression is enlarged when she next sees him indoors. One remembers equally vividly how the minor characters usually appear – the man in the furmity tent with a nose like a copper knob, or the glazier 'a stout, bucket-headed man with a white apron rolled up round his waist'.

Reference has already been made to the original serialized publication of the book. It is clear that this reinforced a feeling for melodrama already present in Hardy. He needed to end as many chapters as possible on a question-mark to stimulate the reader's appetite for the next episode. He expresses this in ways such as: 'The man before her was not Henchard' without telling us who it was; 'You shall be sorry for this, sir; sorry as a man can be!' from Jopp as Henchard dismisses him, leaving us guessing as to what form his revenge will take. Another way in which the reader's appetite is deliberately whetted is in the amount of information deliberately withheld in order to increase the drama when it is ultimately revealed. One remembers the fact that Elizabeth-Jane is not Henchard's daughter; that the lady who befriends Elizabeth-Jane in the churchyard is Henchard's former acquaintance in Jersey; that the visitor at the 'Peters Finger Inn' who subsidizes the skimmity ride is Newson.

The novel is a tragedy and, as Shakespeare found, the impact of a tragedy is increased by a leavening of comedy, particularly if the comedy, as in the *Mayor* has a sardonic aspect. So there is a hard, caricature-like quality about the onlookers in the furmity tent – the auctioneer has 'a damp voice, and eyes like button-holes'. The chorus of rustics introduced in the bar of the 'Three Mariners' regularly reappears to comment on events or on characters. The clerk to the court is gently satirized in his attempts to sound impressive with his 'Hannah Dominy'. Abel Whittle's string is tied round his toe as an improvised but none too effective alarm-clock; the arrival of the member of the royal family prompts the workmen to 'advance their customary eleven o'clock pint to half-past-ten – from which they found difficulty in getting back to the proper hour for several days'; and there is much comedy in the quick disappearance of the skimmity-ride. Lastly, the novel appeals to its readers on a number of different levels. It can be read just for the story; but any reader who is alert cannot but notice the skill of Hardy's descriptions – how he uses telling details like the blue fly that buzzes around the tent when Henchard awoke the morning after the wife-sale; similes like 'the atmosphere suddenly felt as if cress would grow in it without nourishment'; metaphors like the description of Mixen Lane as 'this mildewed leaf in the sturdy and flourishing Caster-bridge plant'; and symbols like the swallow in the furmity tent, or the caged finch that Henchard takes to Elizabeth-Jane and which is found dead. Henry James thought Hardy's style gauche and naive, and it certainly has moments of awkwardness. But it also has many more moments when it catches fire, and then it has an impact that James, for all his exactness, never achieved.

Sympathetic background

Sympathetic background is a device whereby the harmonizing of the weather and the setting with the events in the story at once intensify the atmosphere and broaden it so that it makes the scene into a unified whole.

We meet a hay-trusser and his wife plodding along at the end of a long day's dusty walk, in an attitude of 'stale familiarity'.

The vegetation tones with the two in the story. 'It had entered the blackened-green stage of colour that the doomed leaves pass through on their way to dingy, and yellow, and red'. The dust on the road deadens their footfalls, even as their speech is still; with the exception of the old, weak bird, the birds are silent. Next morning Henchard is a different man, full of resolution and regret for what he has done, and the atmosphere is that of morning – sunny and bracing.

As Elizabeth-Jane paces up Casterbridge High Street on a 'mellow' morning, about an errand that is to end fortunately, she can see 'through the long, straight entrance passages' 'as though tunnels, the mossy gardens at the back, glowing with nasturtiums, fuchsias, scarlet geraniums, "bloody warriors", snapdragons and dahlias, this floral blaze being backed by crusted grey stone-work remaining from a yet remoter Casterbridge than the venerable one visible in the street'.

In contrast with this colourful scene the amphitheatre in Chapter 11 is 'melancholy, impressive, lonely' and in spite of its seclusion, meetings of happy lovers seldom take place there. 'Perhaps it was because its associations had about them something sinister'. Here Henchard meets Susan and later Lucetta – at dusk. As Lucetta nears the amphitheatre, 'The sun was resting on the hill like a drop of blood on an eyelid.' Farfrae's meetings with Lucetta and Elizabeth-Jane are in kindlier places, in a barn and a cornfield. At the beginning of the chapter following Susan's meeting with Henchard, emphasizing the gloom by contrast, is a description of Henchard's fragrant garden.

On the morning when a door opens to release Elizabeth-Jane it is 'fairly fine'. On the day she arranges to leave for High-Place Hall 'a drizzling rain fell', but 'Elizabeth-Jane, having now changed her orbit from one of gay independence to laborious self-help, thought the weather good enough for such declined glory as hers'. Henchard goes to see 'Mr' Fall one evening when it was raining so heavily that ivy and laurel 'resounded like distant musketry'.

The weather for the national holiday of course favours Farfrae. For this and the episode that results in the ruin of Henchard, its role is crucial, moving beyond the symbolic setting for the events of the plot into an area of direct comment on the issues involved. It's as if the weather is taking an active part in the story, ranged on Farfrae's side and taking a malignant delight in Henchard's discomfiture.

The river too is a mournful influence. The town's unfortunates go to brood over one of its two bridges, which even have a macabre hierarchy. Henchard interprets the music of the waters: life ahead of him is 'as darkness itself', as he goes to 'the dark shapes of the Ten Hatches', where the noise of the waters is loudest. 'After night-fall human beings were seldom found going that way, the path leading only to a deep reach of the stream called Blackwater and the passage being dangerous.' Elsewhere the river is called 'the Schwarzwasser of Casterbridge'. It is here that Henchard comes intending to make the pool his death-bed, the dark shade of the river suiting with the leaden gloom of his soul. And when death does finally come to him, it is in a derelict cottage held up by the ivy on its walls.

The Mayor of Casterbridge as tragedy

The Mayor of Casterbridge is the novel by Hardy that has most frequently been compared with various of the works of Shakespeare. The main reason for this is probably that it possesses a tragic hero constructed on a Shakespearian scale – parallels have been drawn which compare the flight of Henchard from Casterbridge accompanied only by Abel Whittle with King Lear's flight on to the heath, accompanied only by his fool. It is known that Hardy saw a production of Othello about the time he wrote the novel and suggestions have been made too that the relationship of Henchard and Farfrae is not unlike that of Othello and Cassio. A writer as widely read as Hardy is likely to be indebted to a number of different sources; but he followed none of them slavishly, and it is plain from his poetry and his other novels that he was more drawn to the tragic than to the comic or the flippant.

The most influential definition of tragedy in European literature is that first set down by the Greek philosopher Aristotle about 390 BC. Writing with Sophocles' play King Oedipus mainly in mind he suggested that the most effective tragedy was when a man rather more good than bad, but possessing a serious flaw in his character, was brought to ruin and death by that flaw; and that the most effective way of bringing about that ruin was by including an element of irony, which meant that an action intended to have a favourable result in fact brought about an unfavourable one. The degree of influence that this theory has had suggests that if it is not infallibly true of all tragedies, it is close to the truth. In the case of *The Mayor* it clearly fits Henchard — a man whose faults are only too evident but who succeeds in winning the sympathy of the reader through his generosity; his willingness to admit that he has done wrong; his attempts to make amends for the evil that he has committed; and the way in which circumstances conspire to frustrate his every aspiration.

Perhaps the largest single obstacle to allowing the novel true tragic stature is the extent to which coincidence controls the way in which events unfold; Hardy himself recognized this. Yet the important factor here is surely that the great majority of these — the entertainment, and Henchard's bankruptcy for instance — are a direct result of flaws in Henchard's character, in this case jealousy and vindictiveness. The tension that Hardy's sure dramatic instincts give to his story helps to give the novel tragic power, and the number of readers who have testified that they have been unable to put the book down once they have started it is proof enough of that.

General questions

1 'Henchard is his own worst enemy.' Do you agree?

Suggested note-form answer

A Atmosphere at start of *Mayor* hints that story will have tragic outcome; sombre, disillusioned. By the time wife-sale has taken place, hint is amplified and confirmed. First two chapters give some suggestions as to how the characters may affect development of story – particularly the case with Michael Henchard.

B Hardy uses coincidence and a delicate balance between character and coincidence maintained in incident after incident.

Examples: 1) The national festival;
2) The weather – visit to Fall and Henchard's bankruptcy;
3) Arrival of Newson – Henchard's lie to him.

Importance of these incidents lies as much with Henchard's own character as it does with a malevolent fate; Henchard to an extent schizophrenic – common denominator between two sides of his personality is passion. Good points as well as bad must be remembered:

1) Readiness to make amends to Susan;
2) Warmth towards Farfrae;
3) Treatment of Whittle's mother;
4) Wedding present for Elizabeth-Jane.

C Narrative refers to volatility, volcanic temperament as well as energy. No one can control his temperament completely. Note Henchard's attempt to keep it rigidly under control in the days of his prosperity by:

1) Keeping to his oath;
2) Keeping away from women while in Caster-bridge;
3) Evidence of real Henchard breaking through even this
a) at mayoral dinner
b) when rustics call Susan 'ghost'.

Henchard doomed by personality, not by chance.

2 'Hardy uses chance as a means of punishing those who deviate from the norm'. How far is this true?

3 Is Michael Henchard a truly tragic figure?

4 What are the main differences in character and outlook between Henchard and Farfrae?

5 'Happiness is but the occasional episode in a general drama of pain.' Consider Elizabeth-Jane and *one* other character in the light of this quotation.

6 Do you find Elizabeth-Jane too insipid to be interesting?

7 'The strength of *The Mayor of Casterbridge* lies in the clarity of its episodes rather than in its overall plot or characters.' How far do you agree with this judgment?

8 'The total effect of *The Mayor of Casterbridge* is destroyed by excessive use of coincidence.' How far is this true?

9 'Hardy's tragic heroes are notable especially for their powers of endurance.' Is this true of *The Mayor of Casterbridge*?

10 Indicate the various narrative techniques used by Hardy in the book.

11 Write an essay on Hardy's use of the rustic chorus.

12 'Hardy's overriding concern is to show the damaging effects of excessive ambition.' How far is this true of *The Mayor of Casterbridge*?

13 *The Mayor of Casterbridge* has often been called a pessimistic book. Is this a fair judgment?

14 'The structure of the novel is faulty in that the period of Henchard's prosperity is much too brief.' Discuss.

15 Consider the part played in the novel by letters.

Further reading

The text of the novel

Since the expiry of the copyright in 1978 there have been many
editions. The most thorough is still the New Wessex Edition
(Macmillan) which as well as Introduction and Notes gives variant
readings.

Biography

Hardy, F. E. *The Life of Thomas Hardy* 1840–1928 (New edition,
Macmillan 1962).

Gittings, Robert *Young Thomas Hardy* (Heinemann 1975; Penguin
1978). *The Older Hardy* (Heinemann 1978; Penguin 1980).

Williams, Merryn *A Preface to Hardy* (Longman 1976).

Criticism

Lerner, Laurence and Holmstrom, John, *Thomas Hardy and his readers:* a
selection of contemporary reviews (Bodley Head 1968).

Draper R. P. *Hardy: The Tragic Novels* (Macmillan Casebook series 1975).

Brown, Douglas *Hardy: The Mayor of Casterbridge* (Studies in English
Literature, Edward Arnold 1962).

Gregor, Ian *The Great Web, The Form of Hardy's Major Fiction* (Faber
1974).

Millgate, Michael *Thomas Hardy, His Career as a Novelist* (Bodley Head
1971).

Pinion, F. B. *A Hardy Companion* (Macmillan 1968).

Vigar, Penelope *The Novels of Thomas Hardy* (Athlone Press 1974).

Background

Lea, Hermann *Thomas Hardy's Wessex* (1913 repr. Toucan Press 1969).

Kay-Robinson, D. *Hardy's Wessex Reappraised.* (David & Charles 1972).

O'Sullivan, Timothy *Thomas Hardy: An Illustrated Biography* (Macmillan
1975).

Atkins, N. J. *The Country of . . . 'The Mayor of Casterbridge' . . .* (The
Thomas Hardy Society, Dorchester 1974) (Leaflet obtainable from
Dorset County Museum).

Brodie's Notes

D. H. Lawrence	**The Rainbow**
D. H. Lawrence	**Sons and Lovers**
D. H. Lawrence	**Women in Love**
Harper Lee	**To Kill a Mockingbird**
Laurie Lee	**Cider with Rosie**
Christopher Marlowe	**Dr Faustus**
Arthur Miller	**The Crucible**
Arthur Miller	**Death of a Salesman**
John Milton	**Paradise Lost**
Robert C. O'Brien	**Z for Zachariah**
Sean O'Casey	**Juno and the Paycock**
George Orwell	**Animal Farm**
George Orwell	**1984**
J. B. Priestley	**An Inspector Calls**
J. D. Salinger	**The Catcher in the Rye**
William Shakespeare	**Antony and Cleopatra**
William Shakespeare	**As You Like It**
William Shakespeare	**Hamlet**
William Shakespeare	**Henry IV Part I**
William Shakespeare	**Julius Caesar**
William Shakespeare	**King Lear**
William Shakespeare	**Macbeth**
William Shakespeare	**Measure for Measure**
William Shakespeare	**The Merchant of Venice**
William Shakespeare	**A Midsummer Night's Dream**
William Shakespeare	**Much Ado about Nothing**
William Shakespeare	**Othello**
William Shakespeare	**Richard II**
William Shakespeare	**Romeo and Juliet**
William Shakespeare	**The Tempest**
William Shakespeare	**Twelfth Night**
George Bernard Shaw	**Pygmalion**
Alan Sillitoe	**Selected Fiction**
John Steinbeck	**Of Mice and Men and The Pearl**
Jonathan Swift	**Gulliver's Travels**
Dylan Thomas	**Under Milk Wood**
Alice Walker	**The Color Purple**
W. B. Yeats	**Selected Poetry**

ENGLISH COURSEWORK BOOKS

Terri Apter	**Women and Society**
Kevin Dowling	**Drama and Poetry**
Philip Gooden	**Conflict**
Philip Gooden	**Science Fiction**
Margaret K. Gray	**Modern Drama**
Graham Handley	**Modern Poetry**
Graham Handley	**Prose**
Graham Handley	**Childhood and Adolescence**
R. J. Sims	**The Short Story**